MAXIMISE YOUR CHILD'S EMOTIONAL INTELLIGENCE

A 12-day Step-by-step Guide

Dr. Sundardas D. Annamalay

TIMES BOOKS INTERNATIONAL
Singapore • Kuala Lumpur

Also in this series:
Feed Your Child Right
Teach Your Child To Read
Your Child, Your Genius
Help Your Child To Cope

© 2000 Times Media Private Limited

Published by Times Books International
An imprint of Times Media Private Limited
A member of the Times Publishing Group
Times Centre, 1 New Industrial Road
Singapore 536196
Tel: (65) 284 8844
Fax: (65) 285 4871
Email: te@corp.tpl.com.sg
Online bookstore:
http://www.timesone.com.sg/te

Times Subang
Lot 46, Subang Hi-Tech Industrial Park
Batu Tiga, 40000 Shah Alam
Selangor Darul Ehsan, Malaysia
Tel & Fax: (603) 7363517
E-mail: cchong@tpg.com.my

Printed in Malaysia

All rights reserved. No part of this book may be
reproduced or utilized in any form or by any means,
electronic or mechanical, including photocopying,
recording, or by an information storage and retrieval
system, without permission from the copyright owner.

ISBN 981 232 089 X

Dedicated to Radamani Arumugam,
for being there throughout my growing years.

ACKNOWLEDGEMENTS

Many people have contributed to this book in diverse ways. I would like to thank the following people:

My mentor in Transactional Analysis, Abe Wagner, for getting me started off 19 years ago—my gratitude. To Jessica Leong, President of the TA Association (Singapore) for providing me with a learning environment. To Dr. Pearl Drego for making me critically aware of the 12 Permissions, which I will talk about in this book.

Gary Yardley, NLP Master Trainer with Excellence, my deepest gratitude for extending my frames of reference about teaching and learning. Gary's brand of teaching and rigour of thinking forced me more than any of my other teachers to re-evaluate my perceptions and opinions about learning in general.

My cheerful life-partner and wife, Chuah Ai Mee, for her tolerance towards my eccentric behaviour while writing this book. To my step-son, who was one of the inspiration as well as test subject of some of the activities in this book, I extend my thanks.

Last but not least, my parents for teaching me about emotions and what they mean. And my surrogate parents for providing me with love, care and devotion.

CONTENTS

PREFACE

This is the second book I have written on NLP, education and learning. The first book, *Awakening the Genius in Your Child*, focused on exam-oriented techniques to improve a child's personal skills and ability. In that book, I had written a small section on Emotional Intelligence. As I delved deeper into the subject, my fascination grew, partly because I realised that if I had known some of the principles when I was growing up, my life would not have been such a struggle.

When I was young, I was constantly in physical pain because of a condition I had. But that's not all. For almost 14 years, I was hearing impaired and had speech difficulties. These disabilities did not cripple me but shaped my life. At that time, I was so dissatisfied with the state of affairs that I promised myself I would master these challenges and move on.

Before I went into practice, I have always wondered why I choose not to accept these conditions as limitations but rather as challenges to be overcome. When I became a naturopath, I found out that my clients fell into two major categories: those who saw their problems as challenges and those who felt victimised. The individuals in the first category nearly always got better and went on with their lives. The lives of those in the second category never improved much.

After working with thousands of children, it became clear to me that children who couldn't learn become easily stressed or fell ill often. Like adults, these children were experiencing emotional difficulties, some of which had to do with how they motivated themselves. I remember working with a junior college student who had brilliant academic results: 5A1s at "O" levels after two months of cramming. However, during his "A" levels, he was not motivated to learn and thus had to repeat the examinations. His case is one example of many children who were academically able but did not progress because they were unable to gather their emotional resources for academic success. Therefore they became mediocre performers in school.

There were also cases of children who were so thoroughly brainwashed into thinking they were stupid, inadequate or inferior to their peers that they never gave themselves a chance. They accepted their low status and continued to do badly in school and afterwards in life. It is indeed very sad, for had these people another chance to build up their self-esteem, their achievements could have been phenomenal.

I have concerned parents who would come to me with their children who had misbehaved. Their misbehaviour ranged from lying, cheating, stealing to violent acts. In most cases, these children had learned their behaviour from their parents. One woman kept complaining about her son who told lies and stole in school. I discovered eventually that the mother did the same things in all the places she had worked before. This is called modelling; her son had modelled his own criminal behaviour after hers.

This book outlines a complete course for children, although adults can also pick up more than a few useful tips here. It is my hope that parents and teachers would use this information in their dealings with children and even in their interaction with each other. Much of the human misery and pain we see arises because most people are unable to access their emotional intelligence. Those who use this book for themselves and their children can expect to improve their personal relationships and environment, achieve greater success and gain more happiness. The book has been designed to be used in 12-days cycles, with each day focused on a particular topic.

Dr. Sundardas D. Annamalay

Chapter 1
EMOTIONAL INTELLIGENCE FOR CHILDREN

What is Emotional Intelligence?
Emotional Intelligence = Success?
Major components of EI
How to use this book

What is Emotional Intelligence?

Daniel Goleman, in his ground-breaking book *Emotional Intelligence,* outlined how our brains influence our emotions. He pointed out that if we understand how our brains work, we will be able to manage our emotional impulses more effectively as well as discover some of the emotional habits we have that undermine our best intentions. More significantly, if emotional intelligence is used effectively, our children can grow up to be emotionally healthier than we are. Besides, improving EI can also result in an increase in all the other intellectual abilities, such as musical or visual intelligences. This is because EI is not an isolated aspect of intellectual ability but a conductor that orchestrates the interplay of all other intelligences.

Emotional Intelligence = Success?

Research has shown that babies who receive encouragement and support have a good self-esteem and are more likely to succeed in life. If you ask these babies to put together two building blocks, they can do so quickly and confidently. This attitude paves their way towards success.

On the other hand, babies who come from broken homes go about the same task in a way that signals that they already expect to fail. Even when they succeed, they have a look about them that implies, "I'm no good. See, I could have failed."

Emotional intelligence, a crucial ingredient for success in life, is shaped by the circumstances in a child's earliest years and continues to evolve throughout his school years. Parents, being the child's closest kin and nearest role models, are the greatest influencing factors in the development of his EI. How competently have you contributed to your child's EI?

Major components of EI

• Ability to recognise your feelings and voice them

- Be aware of the relationship between thoughts, feelings and reactions
- Ability to make decisions, take responsibility for your actions and be aware of the consequences
- Ability to recognise when your heart is ruling your head
- Ability to monitor self talk and catch negative, disparaging messages when they surface
- Ability to manage fears, anxieties, anger and sadness
- Ability to be open in appropriate relationships and know when it is safe to start talking about your private feelings
- Know techniques of handling stress and appreciate mental exercise, guided imagery and relaxation methods
- Ability to empathise with others
- Ability to distinguish between what someone says and your own reactions and judgements about an issue
- Ability to be assertive when the need arises
- Ability to resolve conflicts without being aggressive
- Ability to accept yourself as you are: be proud of your strengths and recognise your weaknesses
- Ability to function in a group setting

How to use this book

This book is designed to be used as a parenting manual. Read through it once, then do the activities with your child. I would recommend that you do one activity a day from each chapter, so that in 11 days, you would have completed most of the activities. In some chapters, I have recommended more than one activity. Do not try to finish all of them in one day; take your time with them. You can always do one or two and return to complete the rest after you have finished reading the book. On the 12th day, take stock of what you have done, and what you and your child have learned. You may want to keep a diary of the activities you have done. Go through the exercises slowly and above all, enjoy them. Here is a summary of all the major exercises.

Day	Chapter	Exercise
1	2	Identify 10 of your most important values. Then help your child do it.
2	3	Practise the Basic Mind Technique, which enhances and further develops your child's mind.
3	4	As a child, what strokes did you receive that was positive and motivated you? What strokes do you give your child that is positive and motivates him?
4	5	Explore the SDI and notice how it affects communication with your child.
5	6	Share with your child the goals that had inspired you. Then ask him about his ambitions and dreams.
6	7	Find a quiet spot and write or record your thoughts on relationships and the people you are strongly drawn to or dislike. Go through the list and see how many generalisations, deletions and distortions you can identify. Try this with your child.
7	8	What stresses you? What stresses your child?
8	9	Discuss with your child the assertive-style behaviours he requires in his life.
9	10	Have your child try out optimal state setting, which wipes out negative feelings, creates positive ones and generates new behaviour .
10	11	Teach your child how to use his skills in the real world.
11	12	Practise ways of building rapport with someone, using calibration, matching, pacing and leading methods. Even though this chapter is dedicated to the teacher and parent, your child can learn how to build rapport with people using the same techniques.

When you have completed the exercises, start another 12-day cycle.

12

Chapter 2

VALUES AND BELIEFS
THAT SUPPORT SUCCESS

What are values and beliefs?
Self-esteem
Values and beliefs can get in your way!
How values and beliefs are formed
Getting in touch with your values
Benefits of value clarification
Injunctions
Giving you and your child permission
The 12 permissions:
Permission to exist
Permission to be oneself
Permission to be a child
Permission to grow up
Permission to succeed
Permission to be important
Permission to be close
Permission to belong
Permission to be healthy
Permission to be sane
Permission to think
Permission to feel

What are values and beliefs?

Values and beliefs are the underlying patterns that give our lives shape and meaning. They guide us in what we can and cannot do. Very often our core values and beliefs are formed when we are very young and unaware of their formation. These values and beliefs have a profound impact on our self-image and how we relate to people.

Self-esteem

There is an increasing amount of research to indicate that intellectual ability is inextricably related to self-esteem. Self-esteem relates to how you feel about yourself as a person, as well as how you feel about your ability to function effectively in different areas of your life. Babies with a good self-esteem grow up to be confident young adults who have the courage and conviction to contribute to society and make the world a better place.

Values and beliefs can get in your way!

In my work with children, I have found that helping them improve their learning abilities with tips on nutrition and learning techniques is easy. Negative values and beliefs, however, are harder to identify and take a much longer time to resolve completely. Very often a person's performance is limited by beliefs and attitudes that they carried around inside their heads from young. Later on in this chapter, as you go through the list of critical values, beliefs and permissions, do not be quick to decide that they do not apply to you or your child. Spend some time deliberating on them; one of them could just make a big difference to your child's learning ability.

How values and beliefs are formed

The formation of a person's values and beliefs normally follow a progression. The three major periods are:

- The imprint period, which occurs from birth to age 7
- The modelling period, which occurs from age 8 to 13
- The socialization period, which occurs from age 14 to 21

The imprint period

The imprint period is the time when we are like a sponge; we pick up and store all information that we receive from our environment. This process is called programming. Our programme consists of thousands of "how to" messages from our parents and significant authority figures such as, "This is how you tie shoelaces." Basic programming occurs between the ages of two to four. We also get our drivers and script around this age. Drivers are messages that a child feels compelled to follow. He believes that so long as he follows these commands, he is fine. Some drivers include "Be strong" and "Work hard." A script is a person's unconscious life plan. It is a plan made in childhood, reinforced by parents and justified by subsequent events.

During the imprint period, your child unconsciously pick up your behaviour and internalises it as his own. This is the time when phobias or traumas and other attitudes and beliefs that profoundly define the child's future develop. I remember talking to an intelligent lady, Sister Lila, who belonged to a religious order. One day she asked me, "Do you think there is anything wrong in disliking men?" To me, this signalled something deeply buried. Under hypnosis, we uncovered a history of sexual abuse by her father when she was barely a few months old.

Many cases of deep-seated dysfunctional attitudes originate at this time. This is known as imprinting. The notion of imprinting came from Konrad Lorenz, a psychologist who studied the behaviour of ducklings after they hatched. He discovered that baby ducks would imprint a mother figure on the first day of their lives. They do this by looking for movement; if something moved just after they emerged from the shells, it would became their "mother". If Lorenz was the first moving figure they saw, they would follow him. Even if he later reintroduced them to their real mother, they would ignore her and continue to follow him. In the morning, he would find the ducklings curled up around his boots instead of in their own nest.

But this discovery does not mean dysfunctional behaviour cannot be corrected. Timothy Leary, a former psychology professor who investigated the imprint phenomenon in man, maintained that the human nervous system is more sophisticated than that of ducklings and other animals. He established that under proper conditions, content that had been imprinted at earlier critical periods could be accessed and reprogrammed or re-imprinted.

Robert Dilts, drawing on the research done by Lorenz and Leary, developed the Neuro-Linguistic Programming (NLP) re-imprinting technique. Using this technique, I have been able to consistently improve my clients'—both adults' and children's—abilities to learn and fruitfully assimilate new experiences.

The modelling period

From age 8 to 13, a child begins to model behaviour consciously and unconsciously. Have you ever noticed how children at that age mimic the behaviour of authority figures around them? These authority figures include parents, grandparents, relatives, teachers and so on.

The socialization period

From age 14 to 21, the child goes through a period where he begins to have more social interactions. The adolescent starts to pick up social values, most of which will be used throughout the rest of his life. At age 21, value formation is about complete. At this point, core values do not change unless a significant emotional experience or specific therapeutic work occurs during this time.

Using specific NLP techniques, for example, through changing the memories from one or more of the three periods, it is possible to alter "inappropriate" values and beliefs in hours, even minutes.

Getting in touch with your values

Many decisions that we make in life are based on our values. Understanding what these values are and being aware of them is the first step towards emotional intelligence. When we are able to identify them, the next step is to determine whether these values are appropriate for us. Outlined below are some values that greatly affect some people.

- To be trustworthy
- To abide by group consensus rather than by individual opinion
- To be recognised as successful
- To be intuitive rather than scientific
- To be able to stand up for oneself
- Never to be afraid

As the above list indicates, there are perhaps hundreds of values and beliefs that influence our lives. The best way to instil good values in children is by example. If adults exhibit consistently good behaviour and are respected by children, they will model this behaviour. But parents must take note that children are impressionable. They may learn socially unacceptable values from other authority figures around them.

The process of value clarification can be broken down into four steps. These steps are constantly interacting with each other.

- Step 1
  Discover what your beliefs are, then clarify, elaborate and expand on them.
- Step 2
  Affirm these beliefs whenever it is appropriate.
- Step 3
  Choose a particular course of action based on these beliefs .
- Step 4
  Act on your beliefs to create a consistent personality.

Activity
Identify 10 of your top values. Then help your child identify his or hers.

Benefits of value clarification

Many decisions become immensely easier when your values and beliefs are clear. Important decisions like going for further education while working, getting married, changing careers all revolve around identifying key values. Clarifying values reduces anxiety, eliminates ambivalences which can arise when you want two mutually-exclusive things. For young children, value clarification will help them overcome low self-esteem, apathy, reduce inappropriate behaviour, cope with hostility and combat indecisiveness and procrastination. It would also stop them from tendencies to over-conform.

When you are able to identify your values easily, it means there are less occasions for doubt and a greater chance of doing the right thing. You and your child would be able to connect with what matters for you. Most of us have a hierarchy of values and what emotional states are least desired. Let's take a look at Jolene's case.

Jolene has a good job in Singapore. Another company recently offered her a position in a foreign country. She has a rich social network in Singapore and her parents still live with her. The position is, however, very attractive. She does the following questionnaire to determine if her values are in conflict. Her hierarchy of values are in the order as shown. Top of the list is love, followed by success, then freedom.

VALUES—What are the things most important to you?	
Moving Towards	**Moving Away**
✓ Love	✗ Rejection
✓ Success	✗ Anger
✓ Freedom	✗ Frustration
✓ Intimacy	✗ Loneliness
✓ Security	✗ Depression
✓ Adventure	✗ Failure
✓ Power	✗ Humiliation
✓ Passion	✗ Guilt
✓ Health	

VALUES AND BELIEFS ANALYSIS

For all of the above areas, consider the following categories:
a. What you must never do to feel...
b. What you must do to feel...

Moving Towards Values

1. *Love* What she must never do to feel loved is to turn away from her loved ones.
   What she must do to feel loved is to connect with the people she cares for at least once a week and let them know that she loves them and in turn be assured that they love her.
2. *Success* What she must never do is to produce substandard work.
   What she must do is to produce good quality work for which she is acknowledged regularly.
3. *Freedom* What she must never do is to put herself in a situation where she has no say in her work or personal environment.
   What she must do is to regularly step outdoors and get in touch with nature or engage in a sport.
4. *Intimacy* What she must never do is turn her husband away when he needs to talk to her.
   What she must do is to communicate with her husband at least once a day and tell him about her day.

Moving Away Values

1. *Rejection* What she doesn't want is to have her proposals or ideas turned down without a fair or reasonable explanation.
   What she wants is for other people to view her opinion as valuable and useful.
2. *Anger* What she doesn't want is to get emotional and lose her temper during work.
   What she wants is to be reasonable and rational in her dealings with people.

After Jolene completed her value inventory, it became obvious that she was very happy being where she was. If she had moved, she would risk violating her number one value, love. She would also risk the possibility of rejection if her ideas were not accepted in the new company. She finally opted not to leave.

Injunctions

Have you ever wondered why good parents produce children with ill behaviour? The theory of injunctions states that children are deeply conditioned by family scenes as well as their parents' body cues and spoken words. Parents are constantly sending silent signals to their children. If these signals are in conflict with what they are saying, it creates a pattern of incongruence that shows up when the children are older. Parents who tell their children "Don't tell lies" and "Don't be lazy" and do not provide consistent models of honesty and hard work are tempting the child to indulge in those behaviours.

Research has shown a comment spoken in anger and frustration is 10 times more likely to impact the child's psyche than a well-chosen platitude. If a father's favourite child, the black sheep of the family, constantly received the message, "What a naughty son I have!" with an indulgent smile, gradually the young boy would learn that he can escape punishment even if he misbehaved.

Messages that you unconsciously transmit to your child contain more emotional power because they reflect your secret wishes, and children obey their parents because they want to please them. Normally the more insistent parents are about social values, the more likely the child will pay lip service to his parents and rebel. Within this framework of obeying to get approval and rebelling for freedom and autonomy, the child's psyche will be programmed for healthy growth or compulsive failure.

Giving you and your child permission

Research in Transactional Analysis uncovered a crucial concept called "Permissions". When we are born, we come into the world with a clean slate with the potential to be anything we want to be. As we grow and develop, we need affirmation that we are developing normally and healthily, as well as affirmation that we are capable and able. Every child needs love, support, kindness and protection. When their needs are met, physical, emotional and intellectual development takes place.

Many parents treat their children the same way their parents had treated them when they were young. A parent who had been physically abused as a child would most probably do the same to his child. If a person frequently hears, "You are stupid", it is very likely that he will grow up believing in it. When he in turn has children, he may pass on the same message to them. If you keep telling your child, "You are clever", your child is more likely to grow up thinking he is intelligent.

Permissions allow a person to live healthily and with vitality and should be naturally given and received. They should not be forced upon your child as an attempt to control their behaviour and thoughts. If, as a parent, you choose to dictate your child's life by telling him what you want to do, then the very spirit of these permissions are defeated.

Consider the 12 permissions below and see if you have received them as a child. At the same time, you can affix the word "Don't" to the permission to make an injunction, that is, if the permission is "The right to exist", then the injunction is "Don't exist". Check if your parents had imposed any of these injunctions on you.

Permission to exist

This is the most basic of all permissions. When a child feels that he has permission to exist, he is welcomed at birth, accepted in childhood and suitably nourished and protected. When you tell your child stories about his younger years and how he was loved and appreciated, the sense of having this permission comes through.

I remember working with a teenager who received the injunction, "Don't exist". She had a low self-esteem and felt she had to apologise for everything she did. She also thought that she could only survive by not being noticed. Her academic grades were at best marginal.

As a parent, you can reaffirm to your child how much you appreciate him in your life. Show him that your love does not depend on what he does and does not do. The best gift you can give your child is the permission to exist. You can convey this by making safety rules about crossing the road. Explain the dangers without scaring him. In addition, telling him things like, "We were so happy when you were born" and "You are really important to us" will certainly have a positive impact on him. Children whose parents have attempted to abort them will unconsciously not have this permission. They often grow up to become adults who develop one health condition after another in an attempt to justify their existence.

A great deal of research has been done to show that outstanding things have been done by people who have had a conditional permission to exist, that is, "You can exist if you ......". Conditions can range from "if you are an outstanding person" to "if you take care of your parents". Some great innovators with a conditional permission to exist were Sigmund Freud and the founder of Transactional Analysis, Eric Berne. Even though they eventually achieved success, these people had to struggle through their growing up years to find meaning and happiness, something your child should not be doing.

Permission to be oneself

In some Asian societies, a cultural bias towards boys still exists. Females are badly treated or even abused, contributing to a cultural ethos that woman are second class. Women who grow up with a sense of inferiority or hating their own gender often end up becoming self-sacrificing, self-effacing and almost totally denying themselves of their self worth and abilities. Boys who grow up thinking that women are inferior and inadequate will treat the women in their lives like property or as subordinates. Telling your daughter, "I wanted a boy when I got pregnant with you" will not make her feel good. On the other hand, telling your child, "I am glad you are a boy (girl)" and being unambiguous about it creates a powerful impression on your child. Your child will consequently not be limited by models of what a boy or girl can or cannot do. For example, don't tell her that only men can become engineers and computer scientists, it will create artificial glass ceilings for her.

Permission to be a child

In today's society where children constantly have exams, there is the tendency to nudge, cajole or coerce your child to start performing like a little adult. Many children no longer have the time to play games. The relentless pressure to get good grades and learn new things such as how to use the computer or play the piano, as well as the lack of emphasis on sports and exercise, can have dire consequences. In Singapore, the ages of children who require reading glasses are getting lower. Health professionals concluded that this phenomenon is caused by an increasing emphasis on reading at an earlier age.

The permission to be a child is to allow your child to have fun and do childlike things while still being dependent on you. If you allow your child to make mistakes and not severely punish him, or if you give him firm guidelines and not push him beyond his limits, then you are giving him permission to be a child. Allow your child to have holidays, where he can enjoy physical activities like trekking or swimming, or treat him to his favourite food. Give him access to all types of information, including information about sex, and letting him know what behaviour is appropriate for his age is also part of this permission.

A child without this permission tends to think he is responsible for others and ends up looking after them. They will grow up to be an adult who constantly craves to be needed, and will encourage clinginess in others. Although such a child may do well in school, it is always at the expense of feeling inadequate and insecure.

Permission to grow up

Some parents never want their children to grow up. They will start their comments with "Daddy's little girl" or "Mummy's little boy". Giving your child permission to grow up allows him the opportunity to be independent and to make decisions, as well as to act his age. Those without this permission may behave like little children all their lives and may never stop being little angels or spoilt brats.

My wife used to encourage our son to help out in the kitchen when he was very young. She did not want him to experience the sense of inadequacy she had because when she was a child, her maid never allowed her to help out in the kitchen for fear that she would make a mess. Although she knew that he would dirty the kitchen when he tried to cook, she was prepared to clean up after him. As a result, by the time he was 11, he could cook simple dishes and even bake a cake.

People without the freedom to grow up are usually weak and unable to make decisions, look after others or play their part in society.

Permission to succeed

In some families, there may be a family script about working hard but not succeeding. So when a child succeeds, he is made to feel unworthy or inadequate. In other families, the parents may think that by setting higher standards, they are motivating their child. They do not realise that they are setting their child up for a lifetime of frustration. I once overheard a mother scolding her quietly sobbing child, "What happened to the other one mark? Why do you have only 99 marks for your test?"

Acknowledging your child's accomplishment gives him permission to succeed. With each step of success, he becomes motivated to venture into new territories and will be driven and passionate about succeeding. These are traits of successful entrepreneurs and trailblazers.

If you have any weakness, do not presume that your children will have it as well. If you have problems making ends meet or being as successful as you would like to be, do not tell your child, "Like me, you will never be rich or successful." Instead, positive sentiments like "You can do it", "I'm really pleased with your work" and "Congratulations for that award" will take them much further.

Permission to be important

Allowing your child permission to feel important gives him a sense of self-worth. Importance is communicated when his needs are taken in account and respected. A child with this permission has few problems performing in public, posing in front of cameras or accepting important roles. They are less likely to get exam jitters or feel that the work they have done is not good enough.

Giving them this permission also means that as a parent, you support their endeavours in extracurricular activities. Not being there on special occasions, such as a prize-giving ceremony, tells them in nonverbal terms, "What you do is not important enough for me to attend." Giving them a sense that they matter will mean that when they grow up, they can function as a part of an organisation or perform in daily life without constantly seeking praise, acknowledgment or public approval.

In the absence of this permission, the injunction, "Don't be important" is conveyed. Such a child is likely to develop a low self-image, withdraw from the public eye and is uncomfortable when attention is drawn to him. A child who is constantly told, "You come from a bad family", "Who do you think you are?" or "You are a bad influence on others" gets this injunction. Some people cope by denying the negative comments and developing a reverse injunction where they are perceived as domineering. These people place great importance on external factors like social status, income and dominance over others. They are easily offended but will not recognise their own offending actions.

Permission to be close

This permission allows a child to experience intimacy and develop trust in appropriate relationships. Such a child can be apart from loved ones without feeling pain and great discomfort.

Being close is easily achieved in some families but is a struggle with others. A family where the parents often demonstrate appreciative gestures to children and celebrate special occasions together will develop this bond. Such families are more likely to raise children who will remain faithful to their mates and convey the same values—"I know I can depend on you" and "You can have close friends"—to their children.

Children without this permission will receive the injunction, "Don't be close". Such children will have a tendency to break ties with some people while blindly trusting others who may betray them. Most of them have broken families or have had sour relationships. Some of them are juvenile delinquents. If they constantly receive messages such as "Don't come near me" or "You are an ungrateful child", their negative thoughts will be reinforced. Research has shown that these people are more likely to experience health problems and reduced efficiency in their lives than those with this permission.

Permission to belong

This permission is essential for your child to feel part of the family, part of the school or part of the club he joins. Telling your child, "You are a part of this family" or "You belong to us" gives them a sense of belonging. When they grow up, they stand a better chance of being successful in their jobs and personal relationships than those who lack this permission.

Children who get the injunction, "Don't belong" will feel excluded and rootless. They may be made to feel like outcasts because of their size, height or intellect. Threats to send them away to live in hostels or with relatives reinforce this injunction.

Permission to be healthy

The permission to be healthy is granted by the experience of physical well-being and the opportunity to exercise, eat healthy food and the ability to handle physical changes and climatic extremes. A child with this permission will be able to take care of himself when he is sick or tired. If you have a healthy routine, you are modelling good health to your child. Paying more attention to your child when he is healthy rather than when he is sick reinforces this permission.

When a child has the injunction, "Don't be healthy", he may constantly feel that there is something wrong with him. He may wrongly assume that he has to be ill before he can rest or receive any attention. Parents who attend to their children only when they are sick reinforce this attitude.

Permission to be sane

If a child grows up in a family where one or both parents take drugs, there may not enough role examples for him to learn how to make firm, rational decisions or receive the permission to be sane. This permission requires the parent to be consistent and supportive of the child. You can grant it by providing appropriate information at different stages of his life and passing on an optimistic attitude about life. Avoid permissiveness and authoritarianism. Let your child know he is capable of solving his problems. Tell him he has boundaries and help him outline them, such as rejecting improper ways of being touched.

Brutal beatings, violent mood swings, and false accusations are all ways of making the child feel the injunction, "Don't be sane". This leads to irrational behaviour and emotional vulnerability on his part.

Permission to think

This permission allows you to trust your own thoughts, process useful information, come up with innovative ideas and make assessments. If you signal both verbally and nonverbally that you respect your child's thinking, he will feel that he is given this permission. When you tell your child, "That's brilliant!" or "What an excellent idea!", you are encouraging the process of thinking and creativity.

Messages like, "How stupid can you get?" and "Don't talk rubbish!" provide the injunction, "Don't think". If a child constantly gets these messages, he would be hesitant about articulating his thoughts.

Permission to feel

This refers to the ability to get in touch with one's feelings and sensations and express them appropriately. Feelings need to be voiced. Some families have a rule about expressing anger. The parent denies the child's anger by saying, "You are not really angry, just tired," or "Good children never get angry". Or he may tease his son out of his anger so that the child never gets to learn to express anger appropriately.

INJUNCTION CHECKLIST

A. Go through the following permissions and ask yourself if you had received these permissions as a child. Tick under A those that you did not receive when you were young. Remember it will be difficult for you to grant these permissions to your child if you cannot first give them to yourself.

B. Next, go through the list and ask yourself which permissions you are currently giving your child. Tick under B.

C. Judging by your child's behaviour, which permission is he still not getting from you? Tick under C.

	A	B	C
1. Permission to exist			
2. Permission to be yourself			
3. Permission to be a child			
4. Permission to grow up			
5. Permission to succeed			
6. Permission to be important			
7. Permission to be close			
8. Permission to belong			

	A	B	C
9. Permission to be healthy			
10. Permission to be sane			
11. Permission to think			
12. Permission to feel			

D. Is your child weak in the following permissions? Tick the ones that he is weak in.

1. Permission to exist

2. Permission to be yourself

3. Permission to be a child

4. Permission to grow up

5. Permission to succeed

6. Permission to be important

7. Permission to be close

8. Permission to belong

9. Permission to be healthy

10. Permission to be sane

11. Permission to think

12. Permission to feel

E. Draw up an action plan to support your child in the areas that are lacking. If your child lacks Permission 1, then spend time with him. Tell him how much he matters. If you find this hard to do because of the prevailing circumstances, then change the situation or get help before you implement the above. Above all, do not say what you don't mean.

VALUES AND BELIEFS

A. What are the values most important to you?

Positive Values
- ✓ Love
- ✓ Success
- ✓ Freedom
- ✓ Intimacy
- ✓ Security
- ✓ Adventure
- ✓ Power
- ✓ Passion
- ✓ Comfort
- ✓ Health

Negative Values
- ✗ Rejection
- ✗ Anger
- ✗ Frustration
- ✗ Loneliness
- ✗ Depression
- ✗ Failure
- ✗ Humiliation
- ✗ Guilt

B. Values and Beliefs Analysis

What are the rules for the above to happen?
For all of the above areas, consider the following categories:

Positive Values
1. What you must never do/What you must do
2. What you must never do/What you must do
3. What you must never do/What you must do

Negative Values
1. What you must never do/What you must do
2. What you must never do/What you must do
3. What you must never do/What you must do

Chapter 3

THE BRAIN AND LEARNING

How our brains work
How to nurture your child's intelligence
Left vs. right brain
Multiplying your child's intelligence:
The 7 major intelligences:
Linguistic
Numerical/logical
Visual/spatial
Kinaesthetic
Musical
Intra-personal
Interpersonal
The growing brain
Teaching your child to read
The reading programme

How our brains work

Our brain is an incredibly complex creation. It consists of an estimated 1,000,000,000,000 brains cells, all intricately related to one another. Each brain cell looks like an animal with a central body and thousands of arms called dendrites. A brain cell may receive thousands of impulses every second. Acting like an enormously complex switchboard, the brain cell will process the information and the dendrites will direct them to the appropriate channel in microseconds.

When a message or thought is experienced and passed from brain cell to brain cell, a pathway is set up. Each time the same pathway is traversed, the resistance of the pathway is reduced. Thus, if you keep repeating a message or thought, a well-grooved pathway will be formed. This is the pathway to mastering everything—from being a world-class ballet performer to being an outstanding neurosurgeon.

How to nurture your child's intelligence

Our brain has three parts: the stem or reptile brain, the limbic or mammalian brain and the neocortex. The reptile brain, which is similar to that of animals, controls our sensory motor functions and survival needs such as food, shelter and protection of territory. If we use only the reptile brain, we will fight or run when we feel unsafe. This is the "fight, flight or fright" response. This part of the brain begins development in the first year of an infant's life, when he comes into contact with his environment. Contact includes interaction with his parents.

The mammalian brain, similar to the brains of mammals, controls our emotions, thus affects our emotional intelligence. The mammalian brain develops around age one or two. At this point, besides growing emotionally, the child also prepares for higher intellectual development through play. Imitation, storytelling, and other imaginative play-type activities are ways in children develop their metaphoric and symbolic capacities upon which higher education rests. By age four, the sensory motor and emotional-cognitive neurostructures are 80% developed.

The neocortex, which takes up 80% of our brain, makes human beings unique as a species, providing us with multiple higher intelligences such as linguistic, mathematical, visual/spatial, kinaesthetic, musical, interpersonal and intra-personal intelligences. To develop the neocortex and nurture these intelligences, several conditions must be met.

- The lower neurostructures, that is, the reptile and mammalian brains, must be sufficiently developed in order to move to a higher level.
- The child must feel physically and emotionally safe.
- There must be a model to provide the appropriate stimulus.

Left brain vs. right brain

Our brains are divided into two hemispheres: the left brain and the right brain. The thinking mode of the left brain is logical, sequential, linear and rational. It is highly organised and though based in reality, it is capable of abstract and symbolic interpretation. The left brain enables us to engage in verbal expression, writing, reading, auditory association, locating details and facts, phonetics and symbolism.

The thinking mode of the right brain is random, intuitive and holistic. It is related to nonverbal feelings, haptic awareness (feeling the presence of objects and people), spatial awareness, pattern and shape recognition, music, art, sensitivity to colour, creativity and visualization.

The left and right brains are equally important. People who favour both hemispheres are balanced in all aspects of their lives. Learning comes easily to them because they can call upon the mode required for the task at hand. If you or your child use the left brain frequently and don't make any efforts to include right brain activities in your lives, the resulting imbalance can cause stress and poor mental and physical health. Try to include music and aesthetics in your learning experiences and constantly give yourself positive feedback. All these will produce positive emotions, increase your brain power and lead to high self-esteem and success. When you experience success, positive emotions emerge, and a vigorous cycle sets in, spinning you higher and higher up the ladder of success.

Multiplying your child's intelligence

When the lower levels of the brain are developed, we can move on to develop and maximise the neocortex's intelligences. The best time to do this is during the first seven years of a child's life.

The 7 major intelligences
Linguistic intelligence

Highly visible in journalists, lawyers, poets, storytellers and political leaders, this is the ability to use words meaningfully. Those who excel in this area can argue, persuade, entertain or instruct. They often play with words and can become masters of literacy. Verbal intelligence is often related to a strongly developed auditory channel. For those whose auditory channels are not as developed, the following activities will increase verbal intelligence. Try them out with your child.

- Hold trivial pursuit parties
- Play word games (e.g. anagrams, Scrabble, crossword puzzles)
- Attend a fun workshop on writing jokes, comics or cartoons
- Have regular storytelling, jokes and riddles sessions with your family
- Read books and comics for entertainment
- Record his thoughts onto a tape and listen to the playback
- Use a word processor to write stories
- Listen to the speeches of great orators, poets, storytellers and other accomplished speakers
- Keep a diary or write 250 words a day on anything on your mind
- Memorise favourite poetry or prose passages.

When my wife and I write, we like to think aloud. In the process, my son gets exposed to our thinking. When he was three years old, my wife would read him stories. When he was about six, she started making up a chain of stories that lasted for six months about a young boy's adventures in space. In these stories, apart from telling him about the planets in the solar system, she discussed what happened when the young hero met aliens. My wife had started this habit of talking to him back when she was pregnant with him. As a result, he currently demonstrates a high level of verbal ability.

During the storytelling sessions, the three of us would discuss issues such as ways of relating to aliens of whom we have no knowledge. Through these discussions, he learned that when he meet new people for the first time, he has to take his time to discover things about them. As a result, he developed an awareness of people that would have otherwise taken him quite a while to discover.

Activities

1. If your child is young, you may want to begin a practice of reading to him. You may want to start with a family storytelling activity, where everyone around the table is given five minutes to develop the story before the next person's turn.
2. When young children are excited at the thought of learning, they often indulge in word play. Encouraging them to keep a personal diary helps them develop their linguistic skills. I kept a personal diary for almost 15 years. So throughout my life, apart from the formal writing that I did, I also wrote in my spare time. This is one of the ways in which the ability to write is fostered and nurtured.
3. Have your child practise in his mind some sounds:
a. A friend calling his name.
b. What he would sound like if he spoke the lines of his favourite comedian, e.g. Jim Carrey.
c. His favourite teacher giving a lecture.
d. His least favoured teacher giving a talk.
   At the end of this exercise, have him verbalise these sounds aloud right down to pitch and tone.
4. Encourage him to keep a writer's book where he can record all his unique experiences. This is the resource book he dips into when he wants to come up with something new.
5. Brainstorming words. For example, use the word "energy" to develop eight related words and phrases:

Power	High Performance
Electricity	Vital Life Force
Hydroelectric	Weak
Charge up Batteries	Dancers

35

Numerical/logical intelligence

Numerical intelligence is inherent in scientists, accountants and computer programmers. Traits of a logically and mathematically inclined individual include the ability to reason, sequence, think in terms of cause and effect, create hypotheses, look for conceptual regularities or numerical patterns and enjoy a rational perspective. Listed below are ways that you can help your child grow in this area.

- Play logical-mathematical games such as Go, Dominoes
- Learn to use the abacus
- Work on logic puzzles or brain teasers
- Keep a calculator within reach for figuring out maths problems in daily life
- Play mathematical puzzles with your child
- Read about famous maths and science discoveries
- Visit the science centre and let your child explain things to you
- Watch television documentaries that chronicle important scientific discoveries and scientific concepts
- Buy a chemistry set and carry out some of the experiments in it
- Identify scientific principles used at home and in the neighbourhood
- Purchase a telescope and use it to investigate the surroundings
- Have your child teach maths or science to a younger child
- Use blocks or beans to teach your child a maths concept

Most people find it difficult to think formally. They have not trained themselves to look at a problem in a systematic fashion. One of the areas of study that focuses in this area is that of heuristics. This consists of a loose collection of strategies and guidelines for problem solving. Mathematician George Polya, who wrote *How To Solve It*, describes several ways of solving a problems. These include:

- Separating the various parts of the problems
- Proposing a possible solution and working backwards
- Describing the characteristics the problem may have
- Finding a problem related to yours and solving it

Visual/spatial intelligence

This involves the ability to think in terms of pictures and to perceive, transform and recreate aspects of the visual world. Photographers, artists, architects, pilots and mechanical engineers will score well in this area. Highly visual individuals often have an acute sensitivity to visual details and can vividly draw or sketch their ideas and orient themselves in three-dimensional space with ease. By going through the activities below with your child, you can help him strengthen his spatial ability.

- Play three dimensional tic-tac-toe
- Work on jigsaw puzzles or Rubik's cube
- Use a computer programme to create designs, drawings and images
- Study geometry
- Learn drawing, sculpting, painting, photography, video, graphic design or some other visual art
- Make three dimensional models
- Learn how to interpret flow charts, decision trees, diagrams and other form of visual representation
- Explore the space around by blindfolding your child and guiding him through the house or back yard
- Study maps of your town and state or the floor plan of your home
- Build 3D structures with Lego, D-stix or building blocks
- Incorporate drawings, photos and diagrams into letters, projects and presentations

With an increasing emphasis on numerical and analytical logic and reduced emphasis on visual thinking, many aspects of creativity are ignored. Perhaps we should learn from people who had experienced the wonders of thinking in visual and spatial terms. Scientists James Watson and Francis Crick won the Nobel Prize in 1962 when they discovered the double-helix structure of the DNA molecule by using a large three-dimensional model as their thinking tool. Designers at NASA (National Aeronautics and Space Administration) regularly create elaborate mock-ups of space modules that save them millions in development costs.

According to Win Wenger, an innovative researcher and creativity enhancement specialist, "What is expressed *by* the learner is 100 times more productive than learning that is expressed *to* the learner." The principle of articulation is that the more your child expresses or articulates his perceptions, the better he will understand that particular perception and other related ones.

You can guide your child through the following exercise, which integrates the verbal and visual aspects of the brain.

Activity

Set up a bright light in a dark room. Have him stare fixedly at that light for half a minute or so, then let him close his eyes and begin describing the afterimage of that light which is momentarily imprinted on his retina. Have him describe its colour(s), its shape(s) and the changes to that image. As he continues to describe and examine this changing image, he may find himself looking at a different kind of image altogether—a face or landscape or other object or scene. Let him carry on describing what he sees, if this happens. For at least 5–10 minutes, keep his eyes closed so that the whole effect feeds back and enriches still further.

Puzzle

```
*   *   *

*   *   *

*   *   *
```

Connect all the dots by drawing four lines without lifting the pencil off the paper. When you succeed, try again using only three lines. The answer is at the end of this chapter.

More mind-games

1. On a blank tape, record three abstract formulas or concepts you want to learn or improve on. They can be very basic concepts or formulas that you first learned many years ago. Leave a silent interval of at least five minutes after each formula. Think of the concept or formula as a work of art that you want to learn to appreciate.
2. During playback, find ways to visualise or experience in sensory rich detail, some form or expression of that concept or formula. Describe

aloud to that voice on the tape or record on another blank tape your experience in hearing that concept. Describe in as sensory rich a detail as you can, preferably with some humour or colourful exaggeration. You can also pretend that the formula or concept is a painting or a music performance, and that you are an art or music critic. E.g. in mathematical formulas involving circles, think of yourself as an inchworm the length of pi, chasing his tail in circles and across circles. Note your observations.

3. If your visualisation needs a bit of help to get going, imagine a closed door, or a garden wall with a closed gate. Describe the scenery and your feelings on this side of the closed barrier. Then suddenly open the door and catch by surprise whatever image is waiting for you on the other side of the barrier. That image illustrates that concept or formula in the way most useful to you. Then play with that image in the same way as indicated in step 1.

Kinaesthetic intelligence

This includes talent in controlling one's physical movements and in handling objects skilfully. Athletes, crafts people, mechanics and surgeons all have kinaesthetic intelligence. Body smart individuals are skilled at sewing, carpentry or model building. They are often hands-on people who need to move their bodies frequently and have gut reactions to things. This ability can be enhanced in your child if you provide him opportunities and encouragement to partake in activities suggested below.

• Join one of the school's sports team or learn a sport like tennis, swimming or martial arts
• Exercise regularly and keep track of ideas that occur while exercising
• Learn a craft like weaving or carving
• Learn yoga, tai chi or any form of physical relaxation
• Play video games that require quick reflexes
• Take dance lessons
• Blindfold your child and have him explore the environment with his hands
• Play charades with your family
• Teach your child how to give you a massage
• Learn typing or how to play a musical instrument

BASIC MIND TECHNIQUE

Below is a powerful technique for activating a series of mental images. This basic technique can be used on its own or as a warm-up for the techniques that follow. You can either talk your child through this procedure as he sits or lies quietly or you can record your voice onto a tape and have him listen to the recording.

GUIDED VISUALISATION

As you lie/sit, be aware of a wave of relaxation moving down your body, from the top of your head to your forehead. Realise how relaxed and comfortable you feel as the wave continues to move down to your jaw muscles. As you become aware of those muscles, be aware of the muscles at the inner corners of your eyes. Then experience the muscles of your eyes going limp. As the wave moves downwards, you feel relaxed and comfortable. Feel the wave continue to move down to your neck muscles. Realise how much deeper you have sunk into this state of comfort and quiet relaxation.

The wave continues to move down to the muscles in the front and back of your chest. Your eyelids become increasingly heavy. Heavier than they have ever been, you become aware of sensations in your body that tell you how deeply you have gone down. You know that you are safe and secure. Know that you are in control of the process and go down only as deeply as you wish to continue your learning. It feels really good as the weight on your eyelids keeps increasing and you find yourself feeling more comfortable than you ever thought possible.

Consider how relaxed and comfortable you feel as the wave moves down to the muscles in the front and back of your stomach down to your hips. You sink to a safe place that you can reach and touch. As you go down, you can use the sounds in the background to take you down much deeper. Be aware of how relaxed and comfortable you feel as the wave continues to move down to the muscles of your thighs. The sounds around you may sound faded. You can use them to help you go down much deeper and become much more relaxed. Be aware of how heavy your eyelids are, maybe 10 lbs, or even 20 lbs. Continue to note how relaxed and comfortable you feel as the wave continues to move down to the muscles of your knees, the calves and finally your feet.

Now your whole body is relaxed and comfortable. Be aware of your emotions. Let them slow down. They are like a vast pool with many layers of different coloured waters. Let this churning pool slow down. You find yourself sinking gently through each layer as it becomes quiet and still. Sinking so gently through the layers until you come to a vast computer beneath all those layers of emotions. That is your mind. Be aware of your mind. Let it be still and quiet. Let your mind slowly shut down its many functions one by one till it reaches its minimal power.

I will leave you for a few moments to enjoy this moment of peace and serenity as pleasant memories very slowly and gently surface, reminding you of all the things you have done well. Feel as good as you wish to about these things. Allow your body and mind to heal as fast as you want to, for this is the state where healing occurs in the blink of an eye. When you eventually return, you may be pleasantly surprised by the many pleasant things that will continue to occur.

Now be aware of the colour violet at the top of your head. Experience it spreading through your body in waves. Let it resonate with a certain tone. What is the pitch of this sound? What does it feel like?

Be aware of the colour indigo at your forehead. Experience it spreading through your body in waves. Let it resonate with a certain tone. What is the pitch of this sound? What does it feel like?

Be aware of the colour blue at your throat. Experience it spreading through your body in waves. This colour is like the colour of the sky or a shade that is special to you. Let the colour resonate with a certain tone. What is the pitch of this sound? What does it feel like?

Be aware of the colour green near your heart. Experience it spreading through your body in waves. This is a rich green, like the green of grass-lands or a shade that is special to you. Let the colour resonate with a certain tone. What is the pitch of this sound? What does it feel like?

Be aware of the colour yellow at your solar plexus. Experience it from the base of your solar plexus and spreading through your body in waves. This is a rich golden yellow. Experience it resonating with a certain tone. What is the pitch of this sound? What does it feel like?

Be aware of the colour orange in your abdomen. Experience it spreading through your body in waves. This colour is like the colour that you see when you look at an orange or it may be a shade of orange unique to you. Experience it resonating with a certain tone. What is the pitch of this sound? What does it feel like?

Be aware of the colour red at the base of your spine. Experience it at the base of your spine and spreading through your body in waves. This is the colour you see when you look at the sun with your eyes closed. Experience this colour resonating with a certain tone. What is the pitch of this sound? What does it feel like?

Slowly switch on your mind's many functions one by one, allowing it to gradually reach its maximum power. Be aware of your emotions and realise how calm they are now. Gently be aware of your body, starting with your toes, moving on to your feet, your calves and knees, then to your thighs and hips, the front and back of your stomach, your fingers, palms and hands, then up your arms and the front and back of your chest, the shoulders, the neck as well as the head. When you are ready, open your eyes. You will feel totally refreshed and wide awake, knowing that your body and mind are working in an optimal state.

Further Activities

Some techniques that would further develop your child's mental abilities are listed below. Do the previous exercise first, followed by these.

Clustering

As an invaluable technique for brainstorming new ideas and finding creative solutions to problems, clustering allows you to access aspects of your mind that you normally access only when you are very relaxed. When you attempt this with your child, you may discover that initially, your child finds it far easier than you do. Here are the basic guidelines.
1. Write the problem in the middle of a page and circle it.
2. If no solution pops into your mind at the beginning, draw circles around the problem and connect them to the central circle.
3. When you finally see a new connection, write that connection down.
4. Work with the ideas as they come up without editing them. Try to visualise the consequences. This will help you generate more ideas.
6. When you have more ideas, you may want to expand on them before returning to complete the cluster.
Now, ask your child to use clustering to find out how he can allocate more time for play.

Problem-solving

Teaching your child problem-solving skills is very important. You may need to demonstrate the following procedure to him a few times before he fully comprehends how to use it.

Identify a problem you may be facing. Write down all the possible solutions that you can think of. You may want to use a cluster. After that, go through each solution and see how your body feels about it. As you go through your list of solutions, give your body response to each solution a score of 1 to 10 (1 being the least comfortable and 10 the most comfortable). Pick the solution with the highest score. In most cases, that is the solution that you are most inclined to succeed with.

Although this method may not always guarantee you the correct answer, you will develop the ability to listen and judge your body responses. I find this procedure very helpful when I work with students and adults who wish to advance to their next level of achievement.

Olympic Mind Training

This method has been used by Russian Olympic athletes before the rest of the world caught on. Now the best athletes like Jack Nicklaus and first-class gymnasts adopt it. Mind training exercises a person's mental muscles and fine-tunes them so that the body can achieve whatever the mind conceives.

Choose a skill or ability that your child wants to improve. For example, it may be to improve your son's tennis swing. Have him experience the best possible swing he can. As he experiences the swing, tell him to be aware of the sensations that he feels in his body: in the arm that swung the racket, the placement of his feet, the sense of the ball hitting the racket just right. As he becomes fully aware of this picture, he can literally step into this mental image and make it that more real. Then he can keep practising this mental picture of the shot as many times as he wishes. As he visualises this, he may actually feel sensations in his body.

Research studies have shown that this mind training technique combined with actual practice achieves significantly better results than the practice alone. A study was done with three groups of basketball players. Group A practised shooting on the court everyday for a week. Group B did nothing at all for a week. Group C spent 50% practising and 50% rehearsing shooting techniques in their mind. When the time came to test them, Group A improved, Group B declined and Group C improved more significantly than Group A did.

Musical intelligence

This is the ability to appreciate and produce rhythms and melodies. Bach, Beethoven or Brahms would have possessed this intelligence. Music intelligence tends to run in families, partly because in such families, the child is heavily exposed to music, whether formally or informally. Here's what your child can do to improve his musical intelligence:

- Sing in the shower or hum a tune while moving from point A to B
- Play musical games with the family, such as 'Name that tune'
- Establish a regular family sing-along time
- Join a church or community choir
- Attend concerts and musicals
- Collect his favourite music CDs and listen to them
- Spend one hour a week listening to an unfamiliar style of music

- Put on background music while studying, working, eating or at during a quiet time in the day
- Listen for naturally occurring melodies, such as bird chirping, or rhythms in footsteps and the noise of washing machines
- Have your child make up his own tunes

Intra-personal intelligence

This refers to a person's ability to access his own feelings and discriminate between the different kinds of emotional states and use this self-understanding to enrich and guide his life. Examples of people who would have this intelligence in abundance are counsellors, theologians and self-employed business people. They can be very introspective and most of them enjoy meditation and contemplation. They can also be fiercely independent, highly goal-directed and very disciplined. To increase your child's intra-personal intelligence, you can:

- Read to him
- Listen to him talk about what is important to him
- Provide him opportunities to develop self confidence
- Leaves biographies of famous people lying around the house
- Have him set aside 10 minutes daily to review his day. If he has no idea how to do it, you may guide him
- Provide him with opportunities to mix with people with a strong self-esteem

When your child is very young, your parenting style is crucial to the development of his intra-personal intelligence. Some parents may choose to ignore their child when he is upset. They do not make use of the moment to get closer to the child or help the child understand his emotions. Such a child will never learn the correct way to handle his emotions. Even if he does eventually, the process will be an uphill struggle.

There are parents who are contemptuous of their child's feelings. Such parents are often disapprove of their child's actions and are harsh in their criticisms and punishments. They typically forbid any display of anger and become punitive at the slightest signs of irritability. These parents may yell angrily at their child, "Don't you shout at me." The child then either learns to become contemptuous of his own and others' feelings or react violently to displays of emotions. In more serious cases, he may be both contemptuous and violent.

If I seem to be constantly harping on the power parents have over their children's emotional states, this is because it is crucial to understand that a healthy emotional functioning is a prerequisite for enhanced mental and intellectual functioning.

I know of a smart kinaesthetically oriented young boy called Aaron. Aaron's parents are constantly fighting. His mother is a teacher who is frequently irritated that the son does not complete his school work. In her frustration and anger, she will scold him, "You stupid boy..." After a while, he began to live down to her expectations. Aaron's father, who has never been academically successful, alternates between two extremes behaviours: yelling at him to be disciplined and condoning all that he does. The young boy, wanting to please both his parents, ends up doing badly in school.

Activity

This is an exercise to help your child work out what really matters to him. Begin with the Basic Mind Technique, then do the following.
1. Retreat for three days. During these three days, have him write down his dreams and discuss them with him the next morning.
2. Have him extract an image from the dream and write down connections that he can make to it.
3. Spend the morning watching clouds with your child and help him become aware of the feelings and emotions they evoke in him. Let him describe to you this beautiful scene in as much details and using as many of his senses as possible.
4. Then have him imagine that the world's most sensitive observer—this person could be an artist, writer, poet, or a version of himself—has joined him. Let him describe this special observer to you as vividly as he can, describing the warm welcoming presence of this most sensitive observer using rich details and the evocative power of his word-picture description.

5. You may want to say the following to him.
"Now using this observer's eyes, senses and mind, perceive this same scene as richly as this sensitive observer sees it, as if you have become him. Then step into the body of this observer, bring your eyes to where the eyes of the observer are, so you are looking at this same scene but through and with the eyes of this sensitive observer. Bring your ears to where the ears of this observer are, so that you are hearing the sounds of this same scene through and with the ears of this person, who is the world's most sensitive observer.
Experience this same scene through and with all the senses, mind and body and feelings of this wonderfully perceptive observer. Now note the differences in the way you perceive this scene. Isn't it now surprisingly rich? Now use the richness and power of your description to make these remarkable differences very real to me. You may start now."

6. "Now stand apart from this observer once again and project on him a warm feeling of thanks. Feel this observer's own warmth at having been able to share such a wonderful and rich awareness flow back to you. With full recall and a total ease, bring that wonderful awareness to the present, making yourself feel very good."

It may be interesting to not only get feedback from your child but to see if, together, you can discover any pattern or any things in common as to what makes the experiences beautiful. Or elicit some expression of the feelings of this experience of describing that beautiful scene— another opportunity to reach for and stretch your child's/students' powers of description and their use of language. You can also gather feedback from him and stimulate further discussion by asking the following questions:

- Did this experience bring you pictures?
- Did you experience much beauty or a special feeling?
- Was this experience pleasurable enough to be worth repeating?
- Did you get spontaneous images beyond what the script asked you to see?

Fine-tuning emotional perceptions

When our son expressed anger or resentment over someone's behaviour, my wife and I would explore why that behaviour brought forth anger. Our conclusion was he often had expectations about how the other person should act and their final actions. When the other party's behaviour did not match his expectations, he became angry and distressed and would throw tantrums and start throwing things around.

My wife had to point out to him that he did not have to react to what the other person did or did not do. He can choose to ignore this person. After both my wife and I congruently modelled to him ways of appropriately dealing with our anger, hurt and disappointment, we saw a change in his behaviour. His ability to monitor his emotional states and function in the school environment with the teachers he disliked improved tremendously.

Interpersonal intelligence

This is the ability to understand and work with other people. It requires the capacity to perceive and be responsive to the moods, temperaments, intentions and desires of others. Someone working in human resource needs to have highly developed interpersonal intelligence. An example of a compassionate and socially responsible individual who was highly developed in this area would be Mahatma Gandhi. People like him have the ability to get inside the skin of another person and view the world from that individual's perspective. They make excellent networkers, negotiators and teachers. To improve your child's interpersonal intelligence, you can:

- Encourage him to meet one new person every week
- Spend 15 minutes each day with your child to help him practise his listening skills
- Have regular family meetings to discuss issues and listen to everyone's point of view
- Spend 15 minutes with your child every day for one to two weeks observing how people interact in a public place
- Encourage your child to watch films and read books about socially competent individuals

Yale psychologist Robert Sternberg and Wendy Williams, a graduate student once did an experiment on several groups of people with varying interpersonal intelligence. They discovered that only a few groups demonstrated a high group intelligence and functioned more effectively than the rest. They also found out that in some of these groups, even though the individual members had only average intelligence, the total intelligence of these groups could be far higher than those groups with highly intelligent people. On the other hand, some groups may have brilliant members but as a group, they could not perform efficiently.

These groups consisted of two types of people: sleeping members who did not participate in group activities and individuals who were too eager. The latter type were a drag on their group because they were too domineering. They lack social intelligence and the ability to recognise what was appropriate and inappropriate in the flow of group activities.

Another study was conducted at Bell Labs, the world famous scientific think tank near Princeton. The lab was staffed by scientists and engineers who were all near the top on academic IQ tests. The study was to identify the star performers and their characteristics.

This was because the work in the labs was often so sophisticated and demanding that it had to be divided among teams ranging from five to 150 engineers. No single engineer knew enough to get a job done. It could only be completed by tapping other people's expertise.

After all the testing was done, the researchers could find little or no difference in the scientists' mental aptitudes. However, the star performers stood out for their ability to develop rapport with a network of key people. These people had a high EI. Things went more smoothly for the star performers because they spent more time developing good relationships with those whose services may be needed.

In a changing social environment when there are more university graduates, it is the socially comfortable individual who will be able to move ahead of his peers. At this point, social intelligence could make the crucial difference.

Activity

- Explore with your child a culture that you are not familiar with. Go through their customs, beliefs and rituals.
- Attend an ethnic festival and join in the celebrations.
- Bring your child to the next wedding ceremony that you are invited to attend, especially one which is outside your culture. Explain to him the unique characteristics of the ceremony.
- Pick a time when he wants to go out with his friends and you want to ensure that he gets his work done. Take him through a negotiation process where he commits to spend time doing two hours of extra homework to prepare for his year end exams. Spell out how you will keep track of his progress and what happens if he does not keep to his end of the bargain.

The growing brain

Scientists initially believed that our brains only developed when we were young. As we grow older, the brain was supposed to stop expanding and the growing process was considered completed, so from that point onwards, we could not learn any more new skills.

A researcher called Marian Diamond, however, discovered after her experiment with rats that this was not the case. In her experiments, she taught a groups of rats to perform tricks. After a period of time, she dissected their brains and compared them with rats which had not learned to do tricks. The rats which were trained had larger brains than those which were not. This led to the incredible discovery that whenever you learn, your brain grows a little larger. The dendrites of your nerve cells (the parts that connect one nerve cell to another) grow longer, so connections are made more easily. These cells grow every time you stimulate them.

So as your child is exposed to more and more information, his brain capacity will increase. As you and your child go through the exercises in this book, you are actually increasing the dendritic connections in your brain and growing systematically. Repeatedly doing the activities laid out in this book will increase both your intellectual abilities.

Teaching your child to read

According to Glenn Doman, founder of the Institute for the Development of Human Potential, very young children can and do read. This is because even before the child is born, when the human brain begins to develop, it is always taking in information. Once the child is born, the brain learns to decipher information, not the eyes or the ears, and is thus able to start learning. Therefore, you can develop a reading programme for your child even though he is only one or two years old.

Doman recommends using white poster cardboard cut into cards measuring 4 x 4 inches. Then use a red marker with side tips and write one word on each card. The word should be about 3 inches high. His advice is to write letters in the lower case, except for proper nouns which always begin with a capital letter. There should be a border of about 1/2 inch so that you can hold the card up with your fingers.

The reason that the reading materials start off with large lower-case letters and then progress to normal-sized black lower-case letters is due to the undeveloped visual pathways young children have. As the visual pathways mature through constant stimulation and use, the print size of the materials will have to be decreased gradually.

Doman feels that children should be started as early as possible on a reading programme. The key to learning and teaching is a high energy and happy environment. Your child should feel safe and loved throughout the process. As the parent, you would need to be organised and consistent. If both of you are not having fun anymore, it is time to stop.

THE READING PROGRAMME

There are five progressive phases in this programme. Below is a summary of each phase.
Phase 1: Single words are taught.
Phase 2: Couplets are taught.
Phase 3: Phrases are taught.
Phase 4: Sentences are taught.
Phase 5: Provide appropriate books for your child to read.

Phase 1

In Phase 1, your child would be taught 15 words that have been printed onto cards.

The procedure consists of holding up the card with the single word "Daddy" clearly beyond his reach and saying to him clearly, "This says 'Daddy.'" He sees this card for no more than a second. Next, hold up the next card "Mummy" and say to him, "This says 'Mummy.'"

Show three other words in precisely the same way as you did the first two. Do not ask the child to repeat the words as you go along. After the fifth word, give your child a big hug and kiss, displaying your affection to him in a tangible fashion. Repeat the above process three times on the first day using the procedure described above. Each session should be at least a half-hour apart and should last only about three minutes. Since children learn very fast, showing him the cards more than three times will bore him. Showing a single card for more than one second will switch him off as well.

On the second day, repeat the above basic set for three times, each session half an hour apart. This reinforces his previous day learning. Then proceed with the next set of five words, which should be repeated three times throughout the rest of the day. So on the second day, you would have given your child a total of six training sessions. Remember to reward him lavishly with expressions of your love at the end of each session.

Doman suggests that you first teach your child words that describe the self. He feels that these words are more relevant to the child and are easier to teach. These words include hand, hair, leg, shoulder, eye, ear, etc. After a week of teaching, you may want to go on to teaching 25 words a day. Examples of words to teach at this point include colours, fruits, objects they see around the home and simple verbs. This should be done in five sets of five words each. Only one set is taught at any one time. Each day you remove a word that has been taught for five days and replace it with a new word. Doman also suggests that parents refrain from testing their children on old words and instead focus on teaching them new words. After a month of teaching, the child would be ready to move on to the next phase.

Phase 2

In Phase 2, the child is ready to learn combining words. At this point, go through your child's prevailing vocabulary and determine which words can be grouped together. If your child has learnt basic colours, there will be many possible couplets you can teach, for example, orange juice, yellow bananas, black shoes, etc.

Phase 3

In the third phase, your child learns phrases and short sentences. The method remains the same: flash the cards in front of him but don't ask him to repeat the words. A simple way of creating these phrases is by adding action to the couplets and creating short sentences like "Mummy is jumping."

Phase 4

In the fourth phase, your child is ready for longer sentences. The aim is not to give him a formal understanding of rules and grammar but an intuitive understanding of language.

All through the different phases, make sure you gradually decrease the print size as your child's neural pathways become more capable to handle higher levels of discrimination

Phase 5

The last phase is to provide your child books to read that would build on all of his earlier learning. Doman, after working with thousands of brain damaged children who later became normal, believes that teaching and boosting a child's ability for reading, mathematics and general knowledge is crucial for overall development. His perception is that parents should not leave this to the school, otherwise the child's innate creativity and potential for learning would not be fully tapped.

Answer to puzzle on page 38

Chapter 4

RECOGNISING YOUR EMOTIONS

Understanding your emotions
Recognising what it means
Self-inventory
Keeping a diary of emotions
How we keep our feelings under control
Strokes
Some strokes sneak up on us later
The stroke economy
Strokes for boys and girls
What depression means to you
What anger means to you
What are your taboo emotions?
Racket games
Trading in bad feelings
Consequences of not knowing your feelings
Patterns that you set for your child:
Conflict
Love and affection
Anger
Education
Work
Money
Bad habits
Leisure
How you can help your child

Understanding your emotions

For many fathers especially, they would not know what an emotion is if it came up to them and bit them. This is because of the way they have been brought up, which is to focus on reason and logic and forget about emotions until they spill over and smother him. By then, it would be difficult to repair the emotional damage. That is why in the previous chapters I have highlighted the importance of being in touch with one's emotions and the opportunities such emotional awareness brings in improving one's life.

Understanding emotions and getting in touch with yourself require a different set of skills from logical analysis or problem solving. You have to be acutely aware of the different sensations that arise in the course of the day and be able to recognise them as they appear.

Recognising your emotions

An average person experiences many different emotions throughout the day—happiness, anger, disappointment, etc.—depending on what happened that day. Below is the story of Mike, who is the creative director of an advertising company.

Mike is a busy man. Last night, he had worked till 2 a.m. and goes to work today feeling exhausted. He is depressed at the thought of having to gather his team to get ready for the next day's presentation. When he steps into his office, his managing director Steve asks him if he is ready for the presentation today. Mike gets a shock. He experiences a cold, sinking feeling in the pit of his stomach and wonders what is going wrong. He has already informed his team that their presentation is due the next day. He brings it up to his immediate boss John, who talks to Steve but with no success. Steve calls Mike into his office and tells him that he had a few days ago sent him a memo by e-mail informing him about the presentation today. Mike and his team are not ready. Steve is not pleased at all and lets Mike know in no uncertain terms. By mid-afternoon, Mike is wrung out with all these emotions.

When he gets home, he is exhausted and morose and cannot bring himself to communicate with his wife. She cannot understand his nonchalance and coldness, yet he does not make an effort to explain to her the difficulties he is facing at work.

His young son, Peter, upon seeing his father, runs up excitedly to him. "Daddy, daddy, look what I have!" he says, proudly showing off his new toy. Mike is too tired and depressed to pay attention. He brusquely tells Peter, "Not now, Peter."

Peter, unaware of the cause for his father's behaviour, can only conclude that for some reason, he is in his father's bad books and that he is not important to his father.

If this cycle goes on long enough, Mike's marriage will be on the rocks and his son will never talk to him again. By the time Mike realises he is suffering from burnout, his wife could be leaving him and his son could have grown up to be a juvenile delinquent.

Self-inventory

The above story is a composite of many families I have seen. What I have described does not happen overnight but is repeated over many years. One of the most common complaints I get from wives is that their husbands never talk to them. On the other hand, when an angry woman tells her tired husband, "You don't talk to me anymore," he is likely to look at her in bewilderment and say, "Of course not. I am talking to you right now, aren't I?" She would then get mad and stalks off angrily, leaving her husband in a confused state.

To solve the above problem, the first step is to acknowledge that there is a communication gap that needs to be bridged. The next step would be for both parties to keep an inventory of emotions in the form of a diary. Once the father lists down all his emotions, he will begin to better understand his own feelings, as well as what his wife and children are going through. Tracking his emotions may not be easy for him, but it is an essential start.

Keeping a diary of emotions

This is the first step towards working with your emotions. A diary helps you keep track of emotions experienced during the day and the incident that triggered the emotion. We can also recognise a pattern if certain words and thoughts generated are repeated. Let's see Mike's diary.

Time	Incident	Repetitive words	Emotions
9.30am	Goes to work	"Same old grind"	Depressed
10.30am	Steve tells him about presentation	"Oh no"	Anxiety/tension Cold, sinking feeling
11.30am	Mike talks to John	"What is going on"	Gets angry about the change
12.00pm	Inquisition	"I don't like this"	Scared, uneasy
1.00pm	Lunch	"I feel lousy"	Depressed
2.00pm	Team	"What a waste of time"	Despair
3.00pm	Tea-break		Self-pity
5.00pm	Day end		Relief
6.30pm	Home		Morose, depressed

Activity

Keep a diary of emotions.

How we keep our feelings under control

Men and women have different ways of controlling or even hiding their emotions. Here are some differences between them.

- Most men do not learn the language for expressing feelings. Women tend to talk about their emotions while men tend to communicate in the language of competition. While this may work well in the workplace in the short term, it places men at a distinct disadvantage in relationships.

- Men do not acknowledge their hurts or losses. Unlike women, they do not grieve and so carry pain with them for a long time. If we bury our feelings, we cannot purge ourselves of painful memories. Talking about humiliation helps to remove the toxicity. If we can acknowledge these past hurts, we defuse their power.

- As a consequence of men constantly trying to control their feelings, they become less sensitive to the feelings of others. They often lack empathy. Most men do not want know how their competitor is feeling because it would make them uncomfortable to know that the other person is hurting. Men who are empathetic often perceive this character trait as a disadvantage.

The following coping strategies are most often used by men:
- They learn to control their facial muscles, voices, hand movements and even their walk from young. Most of them learn not to cry.
- Most men, when unable to hide their feelings, hide themselves. They learn to retreat from other people when they are feeling emotional, to go to a place where they would not be seen. These patterns continue even they are adults. Most men will avoid an event if they believe it will provoke an undesirable response.
- As men become adept at denying their emotions, they learn to deny that their feelings affect them. At first, they may be attempting to fool others. At this stage, they can still sense that they are reacting emotionally. Eventually they succeed in fooling themselves. When that happens, they no longer feel any emotion. They believe they have total control over their feelings. Events may happen but they will be in control.
- As men perfect these techniques, they go on to learn more sophisticated methods. One of them is called the defence of the counterattack. If a man is asked a question that suggests that he is in any way weak and vulnerable, he turns it around so that it seems the other party is actually the one in need of help. For example:
  Wife   : What are you angry about?
  Husband : (raising his voice) I'm not angry.
  Wife   : (gets a little agitated and shouts) Then why are you raising your voice at me?
  Husband : You're the one who's getting angry, not me.

Since young, women learn a different strategy when it comes to coping with emotions. Most of the time, society decrees that women are emotional beings, so they can express themselves. But there are also times when the expression of emotions are subject to the following conditions.

- Some family rules dictate that the women cannot express certain taboo emotions, such as anger.
- Some societies expect women to conform to socially appropriate behaviour. Assertiveness, being a leader in the community or having a good head in business are frowned upon as traits that are considered too masculine for them.
- Some women are expected to make sacrifices for the family. They may feel that this demand is unfair but the feeling is often accompanied by a sense of guilt if they refuse to make the sacrifice. Some of them will even rationalise why things are the way they are.
- Most of my female clients have ambivalent feelings about male authority figures in their lives, including their husbands. At one time, they can experience both positive and negative feelings towards the same person.

Many adults emphasise a lot on being in emotional control. To say what one feels may endanger one's social position. However, an intense buildup of emotions can have serious consequences. It can lead to physical and mental illnesses and tension. It can also disrupt work. Many of my clients, both adult and children, confess to being stressed by demands to perform. Their stress usually arise because they have difficulty living up to the demands imposed on them by others. Sometimes pressure could also come within their own selves. If I ask them how they feel, they describe feelings of fatigue, depression, sadness or anger. When these feelings intensify, ladies often develop chronic fatigue and gastric problems. Men complain about tiredness, tension and being irritable and not being able to sleep or rest. How do you control your emotions? Is your method healthy and appropriate? How does your child manage his feelings? Refer to Chapter 8 for some coping strategies.

Strokes

Eric Berne, the founder of Transactional Analysis, calls any form of recognition a "stroke". It could be positive or negative—an affectionate embrace, a slap in the face or a nod across the crowded room. A stroke is a way of conveying, "I know you are there." The need for strokes is so urgent that children soon figure out that even negative strokes are better than none. Here are the dynamics of stroking.

- The absence of strokes can kill—physically and psychologically.
- Negative strokes are better than none, but they can cause psychological handicaps.
- Strokes that seem positive but are in fact inappropriate behaviour damage the personality.
- Positive strokes that are genuine and appropriate stimulate both mental and physical growth.

Activity

List the positive strokes you received as a child. What positive strokes do you give your child?

Some strokes sneak up on us later

Some strokes appear positive but actually have insidious repercussions. They may feel good in childhood, but later on in our lives, they lead us to do the wrong things at the wrong time. For example, a little girl is constantly praised for being quiet and polite. When she becomes a mother, if she continues this behaviour, she may live up to her name of being seen but not heard and fail to speak up and fight for better education for her own children. Here are some examples of sneaky strokes.

- With looks like hers, she will never have to lift a single finger.
- We are lucky she is an ugly girl. Think of all the worries we won't have when she's 16.
- He is such a shy and studious boy. We won't have to worry that he will get up to any pranks in future.

Women praised for playing victims when young can easily end up as real victims in their adult years. Angela let a strange man into her home, unthinkingly falling for his appeal for help, "A child has been hit by a car. I must use your phone!" Siti was conned into getting into a car, after hearing, "Ma'am, will you please direct me to the stadium?" Positive strokes for submission can lead to tragic encounters. Attackers find submissive women easier prey than their spunkier sisters. To complicate the problem, these women may not move assertively enough to protect themselves, such as scratching, screaming or gouging the attacker's eyes.

The strokes some people receive may also impair their contact with their feelings. For example, tenderness, shyness and martyrdom are commonly approved traits in women; anger is not. Yet in many situations, anger or indignation is usually the most honest response.

Activity

What sneaky strokes did you receive as a child? What sneaky strokes do you give your child ?

The stroke economy

Claude Steiner, an early researcher in Transactional Analysis, proposed the idea of a stroke-deficient economy. He said a emotionally sterile environment would develop if we teach our children these rules.

- Do not share your good feelings or enthusiasm.
- Do not say nice things to people.
- Do not savour a good feeling. If someone compliments you, put yourself down immediately or return it to that person. If someone gives you a stroke you do not want, such as a kiss on the lips from a distant relative, just stand there and take it.
- Do not tell anyone—even yourself—if you have done something you are really proud of.
- Do not ask for what you need. Unless others spontaneously give you what you want, what you have to ask for is not worth a cent.
   All of the above bad habits can be broken.

Strokes for boys and girls

Contrast the kinds of strokes commonly received by a girl or a boy in these situations.

	Girl	Boy
1. Coming home with a black eye	✗	✓
2. Making scrambled eggs	✓	✗
3. Reading poetry	✓	✗
4. Rolling in the mud	✗	✓
5. Dancing ballet	✓	✗
6. Playing tea party	✓	✗
7. Cuddling a baby doll	✓	✗

(✓ means that the child received positive strokes or approval for the activity, while ✗ means the child received negative strokes or disapproval for the activity.)

Now recall the kinds of strokes you have received, or think you have received, in these situations.

Getting in touch with your stroking pattern can generate a high payoff. You can discover more of your script and can gradually change those patterns that are unhealthy for you. But first, you need to become aware of the unique ways in which you give and receive strokes.

Activity

Your childhood stroking patterns

Make a list of all the things that you receive negative strokes for when you were little. Then list all the things for which you received positive strokes. Decide if they made a difference in your life. Mark each item on your list with a plus (positive force), minus (negative force), or zero (did not make any difference).

In the spaces below, list three authority figures important to you when you were a child. They are your sources of strokes. List the negative and positive strokes you received from these people.

Sources of strokes	Negative strokes	Positive strokes
1.		

2.

3.

Now decide whether each stroke was a constructive or destructive force in shaping your life or if it made no difference. Mark each item with a plus, minus or zero. Then ask yourself:

- Who is giving me the same kind of strokes today?
- What do I do to get them?
- Do these strokes feel good or bad to me now?
- Are they helpful or harmful in my life now?

Your stroking patterns today

Look at your life now and think of the various sources of strokes (family, friends, co-workers, teachers or religious leaders). Write down the negative and positive strokes that you get from each of these sources.

Sources of strokes	Negative strokes	Positive strokes
1.		
2.		
3.		

List the people you stroke. What kind of strokes do you give them?

People you stroke	Negative strokes	Positive strokes
1.		
2.		
3.		

After studying your stroke patterns, ask yourself from whom and how you could gain more positive strokes. List the things you do to put yourself down. List the things you do to endorse yourself and think of more ways in which you can endorse yourself .

What depression means to you

All of us have blues from time to time. Depression is characterised by a loss of self-esteem when you are overwhelmed by negative feelings. You may feel demoralised and are convinced that things will never improve, or give up on friends and lose interest in your career. Your child may feel he will never do well in his studies. These feelings are aggravated by distorted thinking patterns, which you will learn more about in Chapter 7.

Activity

What issues depress you regularly? Make a list of these emotions. Identify any mental distortions. Does your child experience the same distortions?

What anger means to you

Suppressing your anger or hiding it from your children can be detrimental to their development. When parents hide conflict, their children will not learn how to deal with problems.

Many people internalise their anger or withdraw from their feelings. Internalised anger leads depression and self-deprecation. These people adopt an "I'm not-okay, you're okay" posture. In the extreme, this posture leads to suicide. Women who learn to hide their assertiveness or silence their feelings of aggression internalise their anger and accumulate resentment. This resentment can either silently seethe inside or be displaced in insidious ways. I have known women who resent their husbands take revenge by encouraging them to eat and drink in excess or push them to achieve more and more till they finally collapse. And all the while to outsiders, they appear to be the perfect wife. People who are cut off from their anger lack skills in handling it. Each time someone steps on them, they suck in more bad feelings. By setting in motion a vicious cycle rather than dealing with anger in an open, healthy way, they are causing more hurt to themselves.

Being aware of your anger and changing it requires an emotional progression. If a person who operates from "I'm not-okay, you're okay" position switches to "I'm okay, you're not okay", his concealed anger will burst. He will blame others for what he is feeling. The government, society, his parents and friends all become his targets of release. Once he has vented his anger, he will advance to "I'm okay, you're okay". Rather than shifting blame, he should focus on problem solving and productive change. For example, Fiona, who was bitterly angry about not being admitted to medical school, eventually ends up working as a legal specialist. Her job is to ensure that women are better represented in medical schools. She also campaigns for equal opportunities.

How do you feel about anger? When and how do you deal with anger? Is it a taboo emotion for you and your siblings? How does your child express anger?

What are your taboo emotions?

Most of us have had certain emotions that we were not supposed to express as a kid. If you openly showed these feelings, you would be punished. For example, Timothy recalls he was once jealous of his sister because everyone was celebrating her birthday. When he mentioned it to his parents, they punished him for the way he was feeling. Lena was brought up in a family that disallowed the expression of anger. If she threw tantrums, her parents would hit her. When she became an adult, she was unable to express anger even when necessary. Kate's mother had a bad relationship once and even though it was over, she kept projecting her guilt on Kate. No matter what Kate did, her mother accused her of behaving in a sexually inappropriate fashion. As a result, Kate grew up afraid of being assertive and not being able to stand up for her rights.

Activity
List five taboo emotions you had when you were a child. What were the effects on you later on in life? What taboo emotions do you now enforce on your child?

Racket games

The kind of strokes that we learn to accept and seek from our collective scripts and authority figures will eventually be associated with a collection of favoured feelings. You probably know of people who get mad easily. Their angry feelings surface almost immediately. Such feelings are called "racket feelings". They mean that a person habitually turns on these emotions, no matter what the situation. This type of feeling is learned in response to difficult or unrealistic situations. It is an early substitute for a feeling that was not acceptable such as, "You shouldn't feel that way!" or "Shame on you for getting so upset!"

Everyone of us has a notion about the kinds of feelings certain transactions will generate. Some people and situations offer guilt while others make us angry or depressed. Once we become accustomed to a certain feeling, we tend to unconsciously go out of our way to find people and situations that can make us feel that way again. Most of us tend to repeat ourselves because we like to maintain a status quo and keep our world the way we knew it.

Mary had a bad racket feeling: whenever things seemed too happy, she would call and talk to her mother-in-law who did not like her. Mary's good mood would then turn to depression. After coming to my clinic, she realized that she did not have to make herself depressed in an attempt to get along with her mother-in-law to keep peace in the family.

John found out that even though he made promises with "good intentions", he rarely kept them. When other people responded with annoyance or disappointment, John felt inadequate. "No matter what I do, it is never right." It took quite a bit of soul searching for him to realise that he made false promises and lied in order to feel inadequate about his own abilities. He discovered this racket feeling when he was on the verge of a successful business venture with a partner. The prospects of being very successful made him extremely afraid and exposed his bad feelings. After consultation, he no longer conjures up these racket feelings.

Activity

List five racket games that you still play. Do the same with your child.

Trading in bad feelings

Our collection of recurring feelings is similar to collecting trading stamps so that we can later redeem them for a prize. If we go after our racket feelings and hoard them, we add to our grey stamp collection. If we gather positive strokes, the ones that make us feel good, our gold stamp collection grows. We save up our feelings and store them inside us, often in the form of tense muscles, ulcered stomachs, swollen joints or tight sphincters. Then when we have collected enough stamps, we "cash in" or exchange our collection for a psychological prize. It is just like getting a toaster at the gift redemption counter! Have you ever felt completely fed up and allowed yourself to blow up at an innocent person? If you had, you were redeeming a psychological prize for your accumulated feelings. You probably even felt justified venting your emotions this way. Different people save up different amounts of feelings before redeeming them. Each of us have our own style, but generally, the bigger the collection, the bigger the prize. Whatever the size, the prize usually involves some justification, leaving you feeling guiltless about the unusual behaviour. Here are what some people did.

- Deanne saved anger stamps until she had two or three pages of them. Then she cashed them in for a good cry.
- Wei Jun saved anger stamps until he had four or five books. Then he cashed these in on a week-long rage at all his subordinates.
- Angie suffered in silence while collecting 20 years of little hurts. Cashing in her drawers of stamps for a guiltless divorce, she reasoned, "Look at what I've put up with all these years."
- Patrick saved his feelings of depression until he had many boxes of stamp books. Then he cashed them in for a guiltless overdose of sleeping pills.
- Leslie accumulated his feelings of stupidity and inferiority, then cashed them in by failing his examinations.

Activities

List five emotions you have accumulated. If you cannot identify them, ask your partner. What emotions does your child accumulate?

Do you express your feelings when they appear or do you save them and then unload them in bundles? Get in touch with how you cash in negative feelings. If you find that you are accumulating bad feelings, develop a plan for handling situations when they occur. Outline your plan. Check out how it works. Redesign it if it is not good enough. Reward yourself if it works. If you have something that needs to be expressed but find it hard to do so, then try saying to that person, "I need to talk with you. Here's what's happening to me. I..."

Or try expressing your resentment about other people to an empty chair. This is called the hot chair technique. Sit down in a chair and imagine the person you resent is sitting opposite you. Develop a dialogue. It may help to start by saying, "I resent ..." Say whatever is on your mind. Shout if you feel like it. If you have the urge to switch chairs and talk back to yourself, do so. Continue until you feel you are done. If you have any good feelings about the person, state them out loud.

Below is an example of the hot chair technique used by Ian, who was angry with his father for dying prematurely.

Ian   : Why did you go so quickly? Don't you know I need you?
Father: I am sorry, son. I couldn't help it.
Ian   : (sobbing) Why didn't you take better care of yourself? I need you. How could you be so selfish and die on us?
Father: I did the best I could. I am sorry I left you so prematurely. You know I loved you, don't you?
Ian   : I love you too, Dad. I am sorry you had to go. I forgive you for dying on me so suddenly. I think I can say goodbye to you now.
Father: Goodbye, son.

Consequences of not knowing your feelings

What if we are too rational or do not trust our feelings? We will be confused about really matters in our lives. If we are unsure of how we feel about our jobs or school, families or community, we will have difficulty working out what makes us happy. I often ask my clients, "What do you like?" They would look at us and tell us all about what they do *not* want in their lives. If I keep asking them what they like, they will look at us with bewilderment and confess that they are unable to think of a positive future. If we do not know how we feel, how can we set clear, desirable goals for our future?

Activity

Imagine that this is your last day on earth. Design an emotional script that would allow you to express all the things you want to say to your spouse and your child. What kind of a life would you like to lead? Step back and look at what you do on a daily basis. How closely does your present behaviour pattern adhere to the above script? What would you keep? What would you change?

Patterns that you set your children

Whether or not you are aware of it, how you and your partner relate creates patterns for your child to follow. If you get things done by throwing tantrums, it is exactly how your child is likely to behave. Research has shown that the way children get along with their peers and their siblings closely correlates with how their parents get along with each other. Children learn to give and take and express their feelings by observing their parents' model of communication.

Conflict

How do you handle conflict? Your strategy determines the pattern that would be imprinted on your child. Do you hide everything from your child so that he never knows that you fight with your spouse? Do you criticise your spouse, from ancestry to bad genes passed down to the children? Or do you attempt to talk out your problems? As the years go by, your children will remember you by the pattern you use most often.

Love and affection

When you demonstrate how much you and your spouse care for each other, you are setting a good example to your children. Dr Theresa Peck, professor of psychology at the California School of Psychology once said, "One of the basic things children learn from their parents is an image of what they expect their own intimate relationships to be like." When parents hug each other, they send a powerful message that they love each other and are happy to show it. Most couples, however, are so busy that they never physically demonstrate their love and affection for each other.

Anger

Children are particularly sensitive to unspoken anger. If they are very young, they may feel that there is something wrong with their world and never grow out of it. A worse scenario is, children from the age of three may feel that they are responsible for the anger and carry the burden of it for years to come.

Education

While many parents pay lip service to education, some have ambivalences about it. These ambivalences can be projected onto your children and can retard their growth and development. One father I know used to talk about his lack of education. While he urged his son to study, he would also hint that education was only for the weak and that the strong-willed made their way to success without the benefits of education. So, his son, in an attempt to please his uneducated father, ended up doing badly in school.

Work

If you only work to eat, then job satisfaction is not necessary nor important to you. All you need to do is find the highest-paying job that you are qualified for and spend your leisure time doing what really matters to you. On the other hand, if you believe that your job should be both meaningful and satisfying, this attitude would be communicated to your child as well.

Money

Is money the root of all evil? Or is the *lack* of money truly the root? Those who have lived in poverty before would always remember the feeling of not having enough. I remember talking with a physician at one of my seminars. He believed that the only people who became rich were those who made "dirty money". A trader I met felt that only bad people made money. So the moment he made more money than he thought he should have, he would lose it all in the next trade. Do you have a struggle with money? What message are you giving your child?

Bad habits

When I talk to people who drink and smoke, they are often unaware that their children may follow in their footsteps. Research has shown that addictive behaviour is often hereditary. Children naturally model their parents and more often than not model their vices while overlooking their virtues. Do you use prescription drugs, alcohol or food to manage your emotional state? Is this a pattern that you would like your child to learn?

Leisure

Whether or not you spend your leisure with creativity and imagination will set another pattern for your child to follow. If you often have mahjong sessions with your friends, this would be what your child is going to do when he grows up.

Activity

Are you setting any patterns for your child? If you are not sure, you can sit down with them and explore the following questions.
1. What does your relationship with your spouse teach your children?
2. What do you feel about education?
3. How do you feel about work?
4. How do you feel about money?
5. Do you or your spouse have any addictions?
6. How do you spend your leisure?
7. What would you do to make the world a better place?

How you can help your child

I often hear a song on the radio and find it both sad and prophetic. A young boy wanted to grow up just like his father. He asked his father if he would play ball with him. His father said he would really like to but did not have the time. A few years later, the boy asked his father to watch a movie with him but his father had to rush off to a meeting. Eventually, the son graduated. The father then wanted to spend time with him but his son was too busy dating. Soon after, his son got married and the father wished his son would spend time at home with him. The son begged off. Years later, the son realised he had grown up with a behaviour just like that of his dad's and began to regret it. How much of your free time do you give your child? How do you usually spend your time together?

The crucial formative period of your child, from ages one to seven, is when you can stretch their mental horizon and expose them to all kinds of ideas. The more mental flexibility you expose them to, the more creativity they would exhibit and the more possibilities opened to them. The capacity for emotional literacy and flexibility has been greatly emphasised in this book. Often, what stops individuals from getting on ahead with their lives are unacknowledged emotions and beliefs that get in the way of their success. The more open the emotional environment is at home, the less traps and problems are likely to surface in the later years of your child's life.

Many parents project their own hopes, fears, anxieties and disappointments on their children. They see their children as a chance to get their lives right all over again. Although this belief is very tempting, this is perhaps the deadliest trap for both the parents and the child. If the child is filial and succumbs to the belief of "father knows best", he may spend years studying medicine in the university, become a doctor and then realise he cannot stand his job. At that point, if he is lucky, he may be ready to embark on his dream. The unlucky ones find out only when they are 40 or 50 that they had never really known what they had wanted to do in their own lives. By then, it would be too late.

How much emotional investment do you have in your child's education or success? Do you want them to succeed for themselves or for your sake? While you are responsible for your child's development and growth, they are not your property to mould as you please. Give them time and space to discover their interests and develop into what they are capable of. This is a right that you too would expect in your own life, isn't it?

Activity

1. Do you explore new ideas with your children or do you stick with the trusted, traditional and socially acceptable?
2. How safe is it for family members to talk about any issue? Has anyone been rejected when he wants to speak? Has anyone refused to listen?
3. How much emotional investment do you have in your child's education or success?

Chapter 5
WHAT MOTIVATES YOUR CHILD?

The relationship awareness theory
Learning your motivations
Value relating styles
Other reasons for behaviour
Altruistic-nurturing ("Blues")
Assertive-directing ("Reds")
Analytic-autonomizing ("Greens")
Flexible-cohering ("Hubs")
Assertive-nurturing ("Blue-reds")
Judicious-competing ("Red-greens")
Cautious-supporting ("Green-blues")
Motivation styles under stress

I am sure you have wondered why your child suddenly has bizarre moods. One moment he is relaxed and fairly normal, the next moment he turns ugly and storms out of the room. He may even refuse to speak to you for days after that. Perhaps you remember how his mood changed as you were talking to him. Have you ever wondered what caused his drastic mood swing? Well, it could be because both of you have different motivation styles and different ways of relating to people.

The relationship awareness theory

This theory was developed by Dr. Elias H. Porter in the 1970s. At that time, many people wanted to learn more about themselves and the motivation that orchestrates their behaviour. To enable them to do so, Dr. Porter created a series of psychological training instruments.

Learning your motivations

The primary tool used to teach the concepts of relationship awareness theory is the Strength Deployment Inventory (SDI) or the Personal Values Inventory (PVI). The SDI or PVI assumes that everyone has a desire to feel valued. By having individuals answer a set of simple questions when things are going well, followed by another set of questions when they are faced with conflict and opposition, their underlying motivation styles become clear.

Through doing the SDI or PVI, the individual comes to see which of the seven identifiable motive sets they use when things are going well and what sets they use when they are faced with conflict. The inventory also reveals how we prioritise these motives as we go through conflict situations that do not get resolved easily.

Value-related styles

The motives that are associated with the SDI or PVI are linked with colours to make recall and retention of memory easier. There are four primary types of people:

- The altruistic-nurturing type or "Blues"
  These people are most concerned with being helpful to others without any thought of personal gain.
- The assertive-directing type or "Reds"
  These people are most focused when leading others towards accomplishing goals and being a risk-taking competitor.
- The analytic-autonomizing type or "Greens"
  These people are through, analytic, pragmatic and logical.
- The flexible-cohering type or "Hubs"
  They are flexible and are capable of leading, helping or analysing.

Besides these four basic types, there are also three blends.

- The assertive-nurturing type or "Red-blues"
  They like to lead when it comes to giving help to others.
- The judicious-competing type or "Red-greens"
  They are assertive. When they lead, they are logical in plans and execution of tasks.
- The cautious-supporting or "Blue-greens"
  They help others because they are motivated by the thought of making others self-sufficient.

Other reasons for behaviour

The relationship awareness theory recognises that there are times when an individual may be forced to behave in ways that are not congruent with their innate motivations. These less preferred ways of relating can either be voluntary and short term as in the service of achieving a valued goal, or long term, as generated by environmental necessities. The theory also tells us what kind of rewards we should give to affirm a persons self-worth and what experiences can diminish a person's self-esteem. For example, while being given a bigger office and more say in staff management would be rewarding to a Red, a Green would cringe at such a reward.

Altruistic-nurturing ("Blues")

A Blue child likes to help others. He is warm and friendly and feels most rewarded when people thank him for his help. He is sensitive towards others' feelings and will always be responsive to the needs of others. He is often very socially adept and is very loyal to his friends and the people he connects with. Such a child benefits most from a parental guidance that is firm and clearly defined. A parent who always includes his children in his activities will find a child in this category a joy to be with.

A Blue child is often unable to tolerate criticism, sarcasm, disloyalty, excessive control, insensitive behaviour or simply being ignored. Sometimes he may be gullible, submissive and impractical. The best way to reward him is to provide a warm, friendly environment and to be considerate and supportive of his activities. Giving him computer games or signing him up for competitive events is not his idea of a reward. Often, a Red father will find his Blue son not manly enough because the child is gentle and caring. This may result in the son trying to please his father by putting on a mask and adopting the behaviour of a Red.

Since he is eager to please others, he may even place the interest of others above his own. At other times, his concern for others may make him overprotect or smother them. Parents who are overprotective may cause the child to be too dependent on them. It is important to help these children develop assertive skills.

Assertive-directing ("Reds")

Reds are often born leaders. They are at their best when they are leading and are able to set goals and direct others. You will notice this even in little children. There will always be one child in the group telling others what to do. Reds are strong, ambitious children who think they are winners and will take every opportunity to prove themselves. They clearly understand that things happen when there is someone to issue an order.

They are watchful for opportunities and are often very good at persuading people. They accept that life is full of risks and are willing to take calculated risks to advance their cause. These are the future entrepreneurs. Reds are also fiercely competitive and do not like to lose out. If both the child and parent are Reds, the competition between them can sometimes get very intense.

Reds would do anything to avoid being thought of as gullible. They look upon those who are not into winning with some contempt and tend to be uncomfortable with people who are forgiving and never fight back since they cannot understand how anyone can be like this. If they have parents who are Blues, they may take advantage of their parents' good nature and boss them around. Sometimes they may be perceived as arrogant, dictatorial and controlling. If they are very young and in a hurry to progress, they may be seen as rash, brash and opportunistic. At times, if they do not do their work properly, they may come across as dreamers.

But Reds can be generous and warm to those who support them and help them achieve their goals. They are most rewarded when they are in an environment that is progressive and gives material rewards. These children can be easily motivated with prizes and badges of rank and privilege. They require constant challenges and verbally stimulating opportunities as well as opportunities for creativity.

On the other hand, if these children are placed in an environment with little challenges, they will lapse into apathy or complacency and become passive and react badly to suggestions or constructive criticisms. They will also demonstrate very low levels of loyalty and self-reliance. The children who fall into this category are either brilliant or laid-back; there is no middle ground.

If this is the major style one adopts when under stress, he will often demand for an instant solution to a problem. If the parents' style under stress is Green, there is a huge potential for miscommunication with their Red child.

Analytic-autonomizing ("Greens")

The Greens are cool, collected, self-reliant and prefer others not to interfere with them. They are also clear-minded, logical and analytical. They value fair treatment and like clearly defined rules of behaviour. Objectivity is very important to them. Greens are cautious and thorough when given a project. They respect the rights of other people to do as they please and will not interfere unless they are asked to. They are attracted to people who tells them what they want without imposing their wishes on them. They do not like people offering them help if they do not ask for it. So always wait for them to ask before you offer help. This would probably be a challenge for you if you are a Blue parent, since you have a caring nature. If you are a Red parent, you may feel this strong urge to run their lives. Hold yourself back.

Greens are serious and conscientious people and are turned off by frivolous people and those who are not serious about life. If your child is a Green, he may wish that he could be more open with people, yet would instantly close up when you reveal your emotions to him. Greens tend to be wary of public display of emotions and are uncomfortable with social interactions. It would be easier on him if you simply present him with the facts and tell him what to do.

Providing them with a computer and a room of their own is their idea of heaven. Being allowed to function in an environment where there is clarity, order and precision is their idea of fun. They derive satisfaction from making efficient use of their resources. Their worst nightmare is to be placed in a unfamiliar place or situation where they are constantly rushed or when events are poorly organised. Signing your Green child up in a football team without consulting him is guaranteed to make him acutely uncomfortable.

Greens are often accused of being cold and unfeeling. Once they have made up their minds after due research and deliberation, it is practically impossible to change their minds. But you have to take note: their attention to detail can lead to obsessive-compulsive behaviours.

Flexible-cohering ("Hubs")

Children in this category have some of the qualities of the previous three groups. They are self-reliant, people-oriented and like working closely with others with clear lines of who is in charge. They are very flexible and adapt quickly to different situations. They are attracted to strong people who are generous with their help. They like to develop their abilities and skills to become well-rounded people.

Hubs thrive is a group setting that is friendly, helpful, considerate and supportive. They are often trusting, supportive, and socially sensitive to the finer nuances of interpersonal relations. Hubs do not like being controlled. So whatever you want to tell them, you have to do so amiably. If they are placed in an environment that is rigid and bound by rules, they would feel stifled.

Hubs may be perceived as inconsistent, indecisive, uncaring and even unprincipled. Sometimes, they may be so influenced by the group that they may come across as having no convictions of their own.

Assertive-nurturing ("Blue-reds")

These children are strong-minded leaders who want to direct others for their own benefit. Blue-reds like to be analyse and think about the consequences of their actions. A friendly bunch, they appreciate being recognised for their contributions. They need to know that they are seen as people who are good at what they do and that they care for others. They are compassionate when looking after others.

Blue-reds dislike being thought of as exploitative or inconsiderate. They are distressed if their efforts to help are rejected. They feel rewarded if they are asked to plan and help organise something at home. Their favourite reward may be a family outing which they get to plan.

Blue-reds are most comfortable with people who know how to assert their authority. They are attracted to people who are decisive and know exactly what they want. If you provide firm and strong parenting, this child will love you for it.

Judicious-competing ("Red-greens")

These are leaders who want to direct others for their own benefit in an impartial and efficient fashion. They are strong-minded and analytical. They appreciate being recognised for their strong principles and they like to organise things in a efficient fashion.

They are most comfortable with people who know how to use power and when to act promptly and effectively. They are attracted to people who will support them and be loyal to them and help them achieve their targets. These children are often self motivated and have clear goals in mind. If you are a loyal, supportive and caring parent, your Red-green child will appreciate you for what you do.

Red-greens like to be trusting and helpful as well as be open about their goals, However, they will only reveal their ideas if they think you are open to them. If they decide that you are not interested, they will not even begin to tell you about them. They feel rewarded if they are given a task that requires resources to be used efficiently to benefit as many people as possible. If your child is a Red-green, let him plan the itinerary for your next holiday.

Cautious-supporting ("Green-blues")

These children are good at supporting others. They are aware of the need of others and will provide support in just those areas. They are warm and caring children who like to use their compassion and mental ability to help others. Green-blues are not very assertive about what they want so they would like to be more outspoken. They are most comfortable with people who know how to use both feelings and reason to help other people and make them more independent. They intensely dislike it when a person depends excessively on them. They also cannot stand being isolated from others or seen as indecisive about their own well-being. They are uncomfortable with people who treat them with anger and disdain. They do not like braggarts, people who meddle in their affairs and those who like to compete with others.

Green-blues are attracted to people who are appreciative of them and their goals. These people should also be cautious in whatever they do for the Green-blues. So parenting that is careful, thorough, restrained and focused is exactly what these children need. You can also help them develop their assertive skills.

Motivation styles under stress

Under stress, your motivation styles can become different. This stress response is derived from your score when you do the inventory. There are different stages in one's stress response. In the first stage, the focus is on the self, the people involved, or the problem. In the second stage, the focus is on the self and the problem. In the last stage, the self and survival becomes an issue.

In my case, when things are going well, I am a Red-green. Under stress, my first stage is Green, my second stage is Red and my third stage is Blue. What this means is, when I am stressed, I would first try and reason my way out. If this does not work, I would start to yell or push my way out of the situation. If this still does not work, then I would give up and walk away,

According to the relationship awareness theory, an individual is always trying his best not to fall into the next stage of stress response. The Red response, for example, gets more and more violent as it goes up the stages. In the first stage of the Red response, people get verbal and loud. In the second stage, some people can get violent. In the third stage, extreme violence can take place.

A case study

Mrs Tan, who was a Green under stress, had a son who was a Red under stress. Mrs Tan's second-stage stress response was Red. When she saw her son turn Red, she would think that she was lapsing into her second stage Red. She would get extremely uncomfortable and would feel threatened by her son's response. In the end, they worked out a compromise: she would tell her son what she was going to do when a problem surfaced and give him a definite time frame after which he would respond.

When my son did the SDI questionnaire, it became increasingly clear to me why he bitterly disapproved of authoritarian teachers and formalised styles of study. He is a Hub, therefore he didn't like to be controlled. He is also not very comfortable doing things alone and needs many people in his environment all the time.

Activity

Go for the SDI with your child and see how your motivation styles affect your communication with each other.
(This inventory is available at Natural Therapies Centre. Parents may book a session with their children.)

Chapter 6

BUILDING SELF-ESTEEM

Build a positive future and have a life plan
Take a personal inventory of yourself
Reward your child
Overcome fears and anxieties
Overcome negative personality traits
Be satisfied with yourself
Be honest
Let go of old resentments
Build good relationships
Assert yourself
Find good role models
Accept help
Learn self-defence
Take charge of finances
Personal grooming and social etiquette
Cultivate good study habits
Learn time management
Understand your motivations
Create a positive anchor
Set achievable goals
Creative visualisation
Initiate one change at a time

Build a positive future and have a life plan

All of us need a purpose in life for our lives to be meaningful. Something that says, "My presence in this time and place is going to make a real difference." For some people, the religious beliefs that guide them would fulfil this. For others, it would be in doing something humanitarian. Many individuals who spend their spare time with the aged or the less fortunate derive a lot of satisfaction.

Drawing up a plan that includes your goals and aspirations will give you a clear direction in life. People who drift through life without a life plan experience a sense of powerlessness and helplessness. When you have a goal, you are driven to succeed. The goal has to be something that matters to you. Similarly, when your child sets a goal, it has to be something that interests him, rather than one that you set for him.

When you have a goal and a life plan, go on to build a positive future for yourself. Believe that life is full of opportunities and it will provide you with a heightened sense of energy. Transmit this belief to your child. I remember working with a young lady, Sharon, who was physically ill and was in a state of depression because her mother had felt hopeless about the future and had not been able to encourage her. By helping her create the vision of a bright future, Sharon became hopeful about her life again. She embarked on many new projects that capitalised on her strengths and abilities.

Activity

Share with your child the goals and dreams that had inspired you. Allow him to get caught up in that excitement. This will develop in him a desire to experience the joy of setting his goals. Then help him name his goals and map out a life plan. Take care not to include your preferences and prejudices in his life plan.

Take a personal inventory of yourself

This makes us aware of the ways in which we have grown or changed. It also tells us whether we have learnt something new or are still hanging on to some bad habits. When your child frequently does this inventory, he is more likely to note his changes. This allows him to appreciate himself for his newly learned skills and abilities.

I once worked with a doctor, a kind man who is extremely dedicated to his patients and very caring towards his wife. However, to his dismay, he found that he was becoming irritated and bothered about his wife's nonchalant attitude towards the general tidiness of their home. After I did some psychological work with him, we discovered that his mother had been a real stickler for small details and he had always felt restricted by her demands. She had never appreciated him for his strengths and abilities. So he has internalised these messages and is acting in the same critical mode towards his wife. After some discussion, I suggested he do the inventory regularly. After some sessions, he managed to resolve his discomfort.

Alternatively, keeping a personal journal will allow you to continually keep track of your feelings and things that matter to you. It records your successes, learning experiences and areas you may want to improve on. It is also a safe place to unload your doubts and fears. Remember not to read your child's journal unless you have his permission to do so. Otherwise you will violate his trust in you.

Activity
Do a personal inventory yourself, then help your child with his inventory.

Reward your child

When you celebrate your child's victories, you are telling him that he is important to you. I remember when I received my 'O' levels results, I rushed home excitedly to tell my uncle and my father. My uncle, upon seeing my results, asked me why I had a B instead of an A. My father was no better; he demanded to know why I had a few A2s instead of all A1s. Thus, throughout my life, I never could reward myself for my victories. If I talked about how well I had done something, one of the authority figures in my life would say, "Don't boast." In the end, I stopped saying anything or even experiencing a sense of accomplishment. This continued till my PhD studies, when I realised something was wrong. With my wife's help, we worked this out. Now my family holds a small celebration whenever my son has accomplished something he is proud of. I do not want to burden him with the pattern of non-recognition. If your child does something wonderful or outstanding, have a family celebration.

The type of behaviour and learning reinforced determines the type of ability a child exhibits. Children will often do anything to get attention. If the only way he can get attention is to be a naughty and troublesome student in school, that is exactly what he will be. Focus on a desired behaviour and reinforce it. Introduce him to the idea of rewarding himself for behaving or doing something well.

Overcome fears and anxieties

Does your child confide in you? If he doesn't, encourage him to. This is one way of ensuring that he does not bottle up all his feelings. If fear or anxiety arises from his inability to do something, then giving him a chance to experience that activity in a safe place would help to resolve it. When I was young, whenever I was frightened or intimidated by something, I would figure out a way to confront it. In the end, all my fears spurred me to do things I might otherwise never have done.

Some children have an active imagination, which can be used to develop a superb memory or worry about all the things that could go wrong. I know of a girl who gets stomach upset the day before her examinations. She would worry endlessly a week before her exams and think about how badly she was going to do. If your child is like her, you will need to teach him stress management techniques to calm himself down. Instead of thinking of the possible disasters that could happen, you can help him focus on all the positive things that would follow if he does everything without exerting so much pressure on himself.

Activity

Ask your child to identify his fears and anxieties. It might to easier to broach this subject during informal conversations. Gently offer him opportunities to explore these concerns safely.

Overcome negative personality traits

Children with negative personality traits generally have problems getting along with their classmates or teachers. Some may even find it difficult to ask for help from these people in their weak subjects.

The first step in dealing with a negative personality trait is to identify it and then replace it with a positive one. The special techniques to be used in overcoming these negative traits will be discussed in later chapters. Help your child to change only those areas that he, not you, is uncomfortable with. Most children will resist what their parents are doing if they sense that they are being manipulated.

Activity

Help your child identify qualities that he is uncomfortable with. Use the strategies outlined in later chapters to help him change them.

Be satisfied with yourself

There are times when we tend to magnify our shortcomings and ignore our strengths. Seeing yourself as you are is the greatest gift you can give yourself. Some adults I know grew up with an exaggerated sense of inability because of the comments they used to hear as a child. One of them, Sandra, was frequently told by an aunt, "You are ugly" and grew up believing it. Andrew's mother frequently remarked, "Why are you so dumb?" After some time, Andrew began to believe that he really was stupid and his schoolwork suffered as a result.

Activity

Ask your child what he thinks are his strengths and weaknesses. Note what he says. The next time you ask him, point out how his view has changed, if it has.

Be honest

Young children learn about honesty by watching others and parents demonstrate honesty by the things they say and do. After working with families who have dishonest children, I realised that these children normally learn their behaviour from their parents who may have told them what they thought are harmless white lies, or in the most extreme cases, covered up their mistakes. These impressionistic children may think that it is alright to tell a few lies because adults also lie. If, in their developing years, no one sets them in the right direction, they would go on to fabricate even bigger lies. Therefore, every time you lie to your child, you are modelling dishonesty. Honesty is a crucial component of self-esteem. It is difficult to feel good about yourself if you are never sure whether someone is going to find out something about you that you would have preferred to hide.

Activity

Ask your child to tell someone a truth and a lie. Then make him compare the two. How does he feel? Does he feel guilty? Let him know the negative results of a lie on people.

Let go of old resentments

Some children grow up to become bitter and cynical about life and people in general because they could not forgive individuals who did unpleasant things to them. Others who are burdened with guilt find it difficult to forgive themselves for their past deeds.

Activity

Before you can help your child let go his resentments, you would need to get rid of your own. One good way is to create some quiet space and write a long letter to the person who has done you wrong. After you have expressed your feelings, you can tear up the letter or burn it. Alternatively, you can try the following yourself, then help your child with it.

1. Get your spouse to listen to your complaints. When you are done, he or she asks you the question, "How do you feel now?"
2. Respond by describing your emotions. Whilst describing, get in touch with more resentments. Then stop describing your feelings and talk about the resentments. After that, resume describing your feelings. When you have finished, answer the next question, "What would you have liked?"
3. Describe your preferences. Then answer the question, "What value or belief of yours did this person violate?"
4. Respond by getting in touch with the values or beliefs that were violated. When you are done, go through steps 1 to 4 again. When there are no more negative emotions, the process is complete.

Build good relationships

Not all of us come from supportive and nurturing families and not all parents show their love openly. In some families, parents do not demonstrate concern but keep it deep within their hearts. Children in such families may end up feeling ignored, unappreciated or unacknowledged.

To improve your relationship with your child, you have to improve your relationship with your spouse and other family members. I have often worked with children from troubled families. The child's self-esteem suffers from the squabbling he sees around him and he may feel inadequate and be unable to perform as a result. So, if you have a relationship problem with your own parents, resolve it before it translates into a conflict between you and your child.

Assert yourself

Children start asserting their identity when they are about two years old. By using the pronoun "I" and saying "no", they are trying to forge an independent identity. Families that allow assertive behaviour without being permissive lay the foundation for fine young men and women.

Activity

Demonstrate to your child the ability to say "no" to drugs, cigarettes or alcohol. You can do this by refusing a alcoholic drink.

Find good role models

Does your child have someone that he respects and admires, someone who is happy and successful, to model? If not, find a role model that your child can look up to. It can be an uncle or aunt or even a good family friend. If he is surrounded by hardworking adults who value learning and education and demonstrate high ethical standards, he will model them. On the other hand, if his mother is a housewife who spends all her time playing mahjong, he is likely to follow her lead. It is also important to have people you respect and admire support you when the going gets tough. There are times when your child may need support from outside the immediate family to support and encourage him. If children do not have positive role models, they may be influenced by the wrong people. But even if your child has a good role model, ensure that he is learning the person's positive traits and not absorbing the bad habits. Every time I watch my son demonstrate mannerisms I dislike, I ask myself if he could have picked it up from me. If he did indeed learn it from me, the quickest way to get him to change is for me to change. Many parents do not realize that they are their child's role models and that their child may be picking up more of their negative traits than positive ones. What attitudes do you not want your kid to model? Work on changing your attitudes because they are more powerful than the words you say.

Developing a strong self image is important for a young student. An increasing number of young people with low self-esteem drift into gangs that promote anarchy and despair. Most of these adolescents derive no satisfaction from their accomplishments. On the other hand, their peers who have a high self-esteem seldom need to take drugs or resort to violence to demonstrate their capability.

Children are easily influenced by their friends. Be aware of the kind of friends your child is hanging out with. Draw clear boundaries for your child. Part of growing up is to keep testing the boundaries imposed on us. As your child grows up, you are going to experience a tug-of-war with him about acceptable boundaries. Tell him that he has to gradually earn his right to widen the boundaries. If he behaves well, reward him with more freedom to do the things he likes. However, if you notice your child has friends demonstrating behaviour that you are uncomfortable with, it is time he makes new friends.

Activity

Invite your child's friends over for a party. This is a good chance to get to know them.

Accept help

Many of us often meet people who are ready and willing to help us. We may, however, have difficulty accepting help. It is necessary that we start to accept the fact that we do not know everything. Hence we have to seek the help of people who are more knowledgeable than us.

Activity

Demonstrate to your child that you too can accept help from him.

Learn self-defence

When I was a kid, I was frequently bullied. One day, I decided I had enough. I would never let myself be bullied again and so took up martial arts. Strangely enough, for the next 15 years, I never have had to use any of the skills. Very often, the possession of appropriate skills provides one with a sense of self-esteem that translates into a positive body language and attitude that keeps off bullies.

Take charge of finances

If your child learns how to manage his personal finances from young, he will be comfortable handling his own money when he grows up. Many people never learn how to manage their finances and encounter many near disasters before they recognise that being financially literate is a useful and necessary skill. The lack of money can often lead to many types of desperate behaviour. Teaching your child how to handle his finances appropriately will create a lifetime of financial awareness and financial security.

Activity
Discuss your child's finances with him. Teach him how to use his allowance efficiently and tell him the importance of savings.

Personal grooming and social etiquette

As your child grows older, he needs to become aware of how to dress and groom himself suitably. Sometimes children learn this by imitation. At other times, they need to be taught. When your children step into society, they are going to be judged by how well they adapt to social norms. So being well groomed is an essential prerequisite.

When relating to other people, being aware of acceptable ways of behaviour during the meeting facilitates smooth exchanges. Teaching your child appropriate social behaviour will make him aware of required norms when he is dealing with other people. It will also prepare him for the larger world. Let him know that different people have different rules of behaviour. This is crucial when he has to interact with people belonging to various cultures. If he is comfortable interacting with people from different cultures, he is never going to feel out of place wherever he goes. Being able to do what is socially appropriate will greatly enhance his self-esteem.

Being appreciative of other people's contributions and making it a habit to thank others for their help is very important. Do you or your family members have a tradition of saying "thank you" freely? Does your child thank you when you have done something for him? On the other hand, complimenting your child when he has done something well is a positive way of motivating him. You must, of course, mean what you say.

Activity

1. If your child needs help in grooming, spend some time going over the use of individual items, staring from the need to have regular baths.
2. Discuss with your child how a gentleman and lady are expected to behave. Then discuss the differences between different cultures, such as in an Indian household, it is polite to eat with the hands. In a Chinese household, one may use chopsticks. In a Western dinner, it would be inappropriate to slurp the soup.

Cultivate good study habits

Children with poor results can feel weak, insecure or inferior. There are many reasons for poor results, including a wrong approach to studying. You may feel one reason for your child's inability to perform is his poor memory. But more often than not, it is because he has a selective memory. He probably remembers which football team has the highest goal average this season and yet cannot recall what he studied in school the day before. If he gets distracted easily, this could be due to an unconducive study environment. His poor results could also reflect his inability to plan his time well. The ability to plan comes naturally to some; for others, it needs to be acquired. You may have to assist him in this aspect.

Learn time management

Does your child feel that the world is a wonderful and exciting place to live in and there are so many things he wants to do? However, his energy is dispersed in so many directions at the same time that he never spends enough time on one single task. Help him prioritise his time. When he learns to allocate enough time to completing each task, he will find that he enjoys what he is doing.

Create a positive anchor

Together with a strong self image, it is helpful for your child to have faith in his ability to study and learn. In fact, the faith in his ability is very closely linked with a healthy self-esteem and a sense of emotional competence. Although this quality can be gradually nurtured and developed, it is often very fragile and can be easily killed in the competitive academic environment.

Most students who have a strong sense of self-esteem are optimistic about their chances of success. As a result, they are often committed to doing what it takes to improve their grades and will be disciplined to do what is required of them. This also applies to children who are determined to succeed. We often hear success stories of students who come from a physically, financially or emotionally deprived background. Because of their circumstances, they are often extremely motivated to succeed.

Activity

This is one way of creating a powerful anchor for him to study. First, keep both his hands on his knees, palms turned up. Then have him imagine as vividly as possible all the activities he likes. Anchor this experience by telling him to squeeze his right fist. Now lower his right hand. As vividly as possible, have him experience himself studying. When he is experiencing this strongly, tell him to squeeze his left fist. Next squeezing only his right fist, have him imagine doing his studies in a pleasurable fashion. When he fires both anchors off by squeezing his left and right fist simultaneously, a new pattern in his neurology is set up, associating studying with the good feelings he experiences when engaging in his favourite activities.

Set achievable goals

One skill you can teach your child is the power to set small, achievable goals. When a target is reached, a positive upward spiral of accomplishment is created and self-esteem is heightened. Goals should be specific and have a time frame. When your child has a goal that really matters to him, you will be amazed at the determination and tenacity that is unleashed in him. Let him begin with small things such as improving his Mathematics grade from B to A and completing his art project on time. Once this habit is developed, the consequences can be far-reaching.

Most students who are not very committed to their school work do not realize that it takes them twice as long to do their homework badly, compared to the time it takes for them to get it right the first time. If your child understands this simple fact and you promise him that he can spend his time doing whatever he wants after he gets his homework done right, you would have created a powerful motive to produce good homework.

Normally it is easier to be motivated about doing homework when there is a series of clear outcomes or achievable goals. Sometimes your child may have thoughts and emotions that distract him from being committed to doing well. I know of a young student who did not want to do well because he would rather remain with his friends in the present class. If you are aware of how your child thinks, it will be easier to motivate him.

A study was done on a class of Harvard students. While they were undergraduates, they were asked what plans and goals they had for their future. Only 3% had clear goals while the others were not sure about what they were going to do. Ten years after they graduated, the original 3% made more money than the other 97% put together. So much for the power of goal setting.

The following qualities have been determined as essential for a child's success both in school and in his life.

- The ability to relate with others on the basis that he will understand them and be understood by them.
- The ability and the opportunity to verbally communicate ideas, feelings and concepts with others.
- The ability to cooperate with others as well as meet his own needs.

Creative visualisation

The more vividly you experience the vision of achieving your goals, the more real your goals become. Studies done with Olympic athletes have shown that their minds could not distinguish between a vividly imagined training experience and an actual training session. This means that a training session that exists in their minds is as effective as a real session.

People with ambitions usually produce children who have high standards. Notice I mention high standards, not impossible ones. It is pointless to set an impossible goal. If you fail to achieve the results you want, your self-esteem will take a beating. Teaching your child how to visualise achievable goals and outcomes creates for them an irresistible motivation to succeed.

Initiate one change at a time

In this chapter, I have suggested many activities. My aim is not to overwhelm you and your child and force you to alter your beliefs and attitudes overnight. Consider these activities as a road map of all the things they could explore. At any one time, just pick one item or issue to work on. Rome wasn't built in a day. Attempting to make too many changes at one go will lead to an overload. It is better to start slow and easy.

GOAL ORGANISATION

An Example:
Long Term Goals
Go to college and university
Become a lawyer/journalist/accountant

Short Term Goals
Get a B on the next math's test
Review the first three chapters of the Science textbook

Weekly Goals
Finish Maths assignments by Friday
Read the first 2 chapters of the Economics textbook
Go through Chinese vocabulary

Daily Goals
Keep assignments up to date
Review lecture notes for tomorrow's class

Activity

What are the goals that your child can set for himself? What are your child's long-term, short-term, weekly and daily goals?

96

Chapter 7

OVERCOMING DISTORTED THINKING PATTERNS

The major patterns of learning and thinking
Deletion:
Simple deletion
Nominalisations
Lack of references or vague pronouns
Unspecified or vague verbs
Comparative deletion
Generalisation
Distortion:
Mind reading
Cause and effect
Complex equivalence
Lost performative
Polarised thinking
Catastrophising
Personalisation
Control fallacies
Fallacy of fairness
Emotional reasoning
Fallacy of change
Blaming
Being right
Heaven's fallacy reward
Internal auditory tapes
Uncovering your automatic thoughts

When people learn, they go through certain patterns of thinking and information processing. In this chapter, we will deal with the structure of learning and thinking as reflected in our language.

The major patterns of learning and thinking

There are three learning processes: deletion, generalisation and distortion. All the information that we take in is influenced by three constraints or filters. Knowing how these filters work will help us better understand ourselves and the people we interact with. The three filters are neurological, social and individual.

When we take in information through our neurological systems or sensory organs and nerves, depending on the make-up of your body, this information is translated into signals. This explains why the same event can have different meanings to different people; no one reacts to the world at large; we only respond to our personal model of the world.

Our social and cultural differences also account for differences in our model. This is the second level filter. The primary example of social constraints is language, which may enhance or limit our perception. When we use a language, we encode what we perceive into labels and words which our minds manipulate to make sense of them. For example, snow is so important to Eskimos that they have 70 different words for the different types of snow. People who come from other linguistic backgrounds will probably not be able to be aware of the differences. There are other aspect of social constraints that affect a person's internal modelling process. These include the society he lives in, its institutions, traditions, values, beliefs, ideas and technologies, as well as his immediate family and friends.

Social conventions are learned and integrated by an individual in the same way a language is learned. For example, Malaysia is a culture that highly values respect and politeness. Those who are exposed to an intolerable level of stress could exhibit a form of hysterical behaviour that had quasi-spiritual overtones called "running amok". This provides an acceptable outlet for behaviour that included being aggressive, unrestrained and unconstrained by the normal social conventions.

Lastly, individual constraint arise as a result of the person's past experiences. Individual constraints include both neurological and social constraints. They play an important part in shaping individual experience and interpretation, like the different reactions of an optimist and a pessimist in an identical situation.

Language is one of the primary ways we use to interact among ourselves and with other people. When Singaporeans speak English, we tend to leave out certain bits of information. Another English speaker would have to use his intuitive sense of the language and "enter" our heads to make sense of what we are saying. We can also say that he is systematically deleting, generalising or distorting the information that is presented to him.

Deletion

The human nervous system is being fed more than two million pieces of information every second. To cope with this, it operates a filtering mechanism that enables us to function at maximum efficiency. What comes out is a significantly reduced amount of information that is sufficient for our daily survival. There are five types of deletion.

Simple deletion

Read the following sentences:

Malaysia in the the monsoon.

The quick brown fox jumped over the the lazy dog.

When you look at the above sentences, most people will make sense of the above by deleting information that does not make sense. Did you realised the extra "the" in the sentences above? Many people only realise their existence after they have been pointed out. When these same habits are carried over into communication and interpersonal relations, the consequences can be devastating. Those who are often depressed delete from their memory all their happy times. They only retain memories of depression. If I make them laugh at a joke, distract them and then point out that they laughed, they will often say, "Oh, I was not really laughing. I was only going through the motions."

Nominalisations

In this category, the person changes an active verb into a frozen noun. Verbs that are often misused this way are failing (failure), relating (relationship) and deciding (decision). To make things clearer, let us look at the following examples.

Your child has been having difficulty in mathematics. He comes home one day and tells you, "I am a failure." You ask, "In what way are you failing?" He explains, "I do not know how to multiply." By asking the above question, you have identified your child's problem area and changed the noun "failure" to a verb "failing". If he cannot multiply, he can now learn how to. When he says he is a failure, it means the fact cannot be changed. The two words have a world of difference.

Take another example. Your child says, "My class teacher and I have a bad relationship." You ask, "How is the way you are relating bad?" He answers, "I get little satisfaction." So you ask again, "What specifically would be more satisfying?" This way, you can both start looking at other ways your child can relate to his class teacher.

Lack of references or vague pronouns

Sometime, essential information is left out in conversations because the speaker assumes everyone has all the information. For example, your child storms home angrily one day and says, "She did it again!" You ask, "Who did what again?" You need to find out exactly what has happened. Or he says, "My teachers treat me unfairly." You ask, "Which specific teachers are unfair to you?" This way, your child has to decide if it is a few teachers or just one who is unfair. You could further determine what his definition of "unfair" is.

Unspecified or vague verbs

Your child may sometimes be bursting with emotions about a situation that he is not sure about. "I am angry," he says. You ask, "What are you angry about?" In attempting to answer this question, he may discover that his emotions may have nothing to do with the situation at all.

Comparative deletion

Parents, teachers and children are always making comparisons. In doing so, they often lose a sense of perspective. When examinations draw near and my son grows desperate, he would often hurl these lines at me, "I am not very smart," or "I am stupid." He feels that if he is inadequate, he has a good reason to carry on his bad study habits. To steer him back to the right direction, I usually ask him, "Compared to whom?" or "Compared to what?" That usually stops him from making comparisons.

Generalisations

We may sometimes encounter someone with a rigid sense of what they can or cannot do. They may not even be aware that they are limiting their options. For example, your child says, "I can never get it right." So you ask, "You have never, ever got it right?" Usually, if this question is asked, most people will remember at least one time when they got things right.

Distortion

The last category refers to how we personally make sense of things by personalising information to fit our own model of the world. In other words, we distort information to make it fit into our perception.

Mind reading

This happens when someone believes that he knows at some level what the other person is thinking. He will often disregard information that contradicts what they believe. Mind readers often make assumptions about how other people feel and what motivates them. Children sometimes mind reads their teachers. Parents who tend to over-control their children may also do this. If someone tells you, "I know what you are thinking," ask him, "How do you know?"

Cause and effect

This surfaces when someone believes that someone else is responsible for the way they feel. This is a fallacy and allows the first person not to take responsibility for his feelings. Asking him the right questions will help him remove this set of beliefs. For example, when someone says, "You make me angry," ask, "How do I make you angry?" If your child says, "When I pass my exams, I will be smart," ask him, "Is everyone who has passed the exams smart?"

Complex equivalence

This distortion forms when two entirely different qualities are linked to each other. For example, teachers may believe that students should look at them when they are talking to them, implying the following:

Looking at me = Paying attention to what I am saying

This may not be true for students who learn by auditory methods. Another common complex equivalence is, if you are interested in your schoolwork, you will pay attention in class.

Interested in your schoolwork = Paying attention in class

Lost performative

Lost performatives refers to judgements, beliefs and standards that have been around for so long that people have forgotten where they came from or if they are still valid. They often are generalisations about the world and may have no real connections with the situation at hand. They also reflect deep-seated cultural beliefs and ideas. When faced with lost performatives, you should be sceptical and ask, "Who said this?"

Examples of lost performatives are:
- A strong man is always in control.
- She is a good woman. She never complains about her suffering.
- Fooling around is fine for men but a decent woman would not do it.
- A woman's place is at home.

Polarised thinking

In polarised thinking, everything is either wonderful or downright horrible; there is no room for the middle ground. For example, if you are less than perfect or not exceptionally brilliant at any time, then you must be a failure. The real danger in this thinking pattern is, there is no room for mistakes and mediocrity. This creates a lot of stress and constantly attacks one's self-esteem.

The solution is to tell yourself or your child that there are very few absolutes. Start thinking of your feelings in percentage terms. Remember at most times, you have mixed feelings. For example, when you are watching a horror movie, you are not 100% scared, only 70% scared; the other 30% is curiosity about what will happen next.

Catastrophising

Catastrophising is when you take a small incident like doing badly in a test and, by a chain of thoughts, blow it up into a life or death situation. One of my clients told me how as a student, he would worry about failing a test. He reasoned that if he failed the test, he would fail his exams and not be able to go to college and university, which means he cannot get a degree. His whole life would be ruined as a result. The solution is to make a realistic appraisal of the odds. This way, you can always strive to change the odds in your favour.

Personalisation

When someone attempts a personalisation, they make themselves the centre of the world. Everything that happens is related to them. When you start personalising and hear your child say he is tired, you would feel he is tired of you. If your spouse complains about the rising cost of living, you would see it as an attack on you for not earning enough.

The solution is to check the validity of your conclusions. Is your teacher really angry with you? Are your friends really looking down on you? Make no conclusions until there is sufficient evidence. Stop playing with your self-esteem.

Control fallacies

There are two ways a person can distort his sense of control. In the first way, he sees himself as omnipotent and responsible for everyone around him. In the second way, he sees himself as helpless and out of control.

If you tend to have control fallacies, first realise that everyone is responsible for their lives and their own actions. If someone experiences physical or emotional discomfort, it is their own responsibility.

Fallacy of fairness

This hinges on the application of rules to the vagaries of interpersonal relations. Since different people have different standards of fairness, there is often no third party to turn to. The solution is to say what you want or prefer without dressing it up or pretending to be fair.

Emotional reasoning

Emotional reasoning occurs when you feel that your belief must be true. If you feel you are a loser, then you *must* be a loser. If you feel guilty, then you *must* be guilty. The problem with emotional reasoning is that beliefs by themselves cannot measure what is happening around you. They are sometimes products of distorted thinking. If your beliefs are distorted, your emotions will reflect these distortions.

The solution is to understand that your feelings may not always accurately reflect what is going on around you. There is nothing that says that whatever you feel must be true. Look at your feelings sceptically.

Fallacy of change

The fallacy of change is the belief that by putting enough pressure on other people, they will change. So all the energy and attention is focused on getting them to meet your needs. Ways of changing others include demanding, withholding and trading. The common result is, the recipient feels attacked or pushed around and does not change at all.

The solution is to take responsibility and go for what you want or do not want instead of changing others to accommodate your needs. In reality, the only person we can really change is ourselves.

Blaming

Blaming means making someone else responsible for your decisions. It often means telling yourself that others are responsible for your pain, misery or discomfort. Violent people habitually blame others for triggering their violence.

The solution is to realise that we are responsible for ourselves and our actions. We can choose to make ourselves happy or sad. It is our own responsibility to assert our needs or make a decision.

Being right

In this distortion, you continually strive to prove that your viewpoint is correct and everything you do is right. You are not interested in others being right; you are only keen on defending your own stand.

Try to listen to others. If you do, you may discover many things that would lead you to conclude that you are not infallible; there are times when you can be wrong too.

Heaven's reward fallacy

This means that you believe if you always do the right thing, eventually you will be rewarded. You sacrifice and slog all your life and imagine that you are collecting gold stars that you can cash in one day.

However, this thinking is not correct. The time to live and reward yourself is now. The nature of your relationships and the way you are progressing towards your goals are all part of the reward.

Internal auditory tapes

Research has shown that everyone has different ways of communicating with ourselves. Some of us have repetitive feelings, some keep seeing recurrent pictures in their minds while others may keep hearing a variety of internal dialogue. Of these, the last one, known as internal auditory tapes, seems to be the most recurrent in generating negative images and feelings.

Such messages are normally parental or guardian figure injunctions that we keep generating at certain stress points in our lives. Depending on your nature, such stress points may come up very often. A rather disconcerting fact is, these internal messages are often beyond your conscious awareness or have become so habitual that they seem to be a part of you rather than a habit that you have cultivated.

Uncovering your automatic thoughts

We all have a range of prerecorded conversations or self talk that we keep playing back to ourselves. These thoughts support the values and beliefs we have and our status quo.

Activity

Find a quiet spot and write or record on a tape a short passage about something that you strongly believe in or strongly oppose. Next, write or record down your feelings of people whom you are strongly drawn to or whom you intensely dislike. After that, go through what you have written or recorded and see how many deletions, generalisations and distortions you can identify. Every time you go through this activity, you may just work with one category. For example, you may want to work on your deletions the first time you do this activity. In the second 12-day cycle, you may choose to identify your generalisations, and so on. Help your child with this activity.

Chapter 8

COPING WITH STRESS

Some causes of stress for children
Why we should teach our children lifeskills
Life in the concrete jungle
Lifeskills development
Short-term and long-term stress
Effects of short-term stress
Effects of long-term stress
How a person's stress response develops
How stress is aggravated
How stress is defused
Coping with stress:
Keep fit
Stay cool
Learn to read the environment
Managing stressful situations

As an adult, you can easily recognise stress. But how do you deal with it? Different people have different ways of coping with stress, ranging from drinking coffee to retreating to a quiet corner or even falling sick. These coping techniques provide us some relief by distracting or disengaging us from a potentially stressful situation. However, some forms of coping are unhealthy and destructive, such as alcoholism or taking drugs for adults, or truancy, hanging out with gangs or deliberately performing badly in school for children.

One of the most powerful ways children learn is by watching what significant adult role-models in their lives do in different situations, then model these behaviours. As a parent, it may distress you to note that they may not only model your positive behaviour but also your inappropriate stress-coping strategy. A parent who loses his temper under stress may unconsciously teach his child that this is the way to behave. Another who consumes alcoholic drinks to relax may be teaching his child that alcohol is one of the best ways of unwinding.

While some people handle stress badly, there are others who use the right techniques to cope with stress. They will identify the causes of their stress and their personal stress signals, then frequently monitor their stress level and develop ways to cope with it.

The techniques introduced in this chapter will lay the foundation for maintaining a high energy level and self-esteem under stress, which will directly enhance academic performance. This is crucial for success and overall performance in school. In the first seven chapters, we have explored the different skills that would enhance your child's grades; in this chapter, we will look at other skills that would ensure that the earlier mentioned skills can be used effectively.

These skills include techniques to reduce stress and anxiety, ranging from effective time management and goal achievement to setting up healthy social networks and learning ways of asserting yourself. Children who develop these skills will normally be able to take care of themselves physically and emotionally.

Some causes of stress for children

- My parents expect me to be perfect.
- My parents insist my grades are never good enough.
- My teachers have impossible expectations.
- My parents expect me to have perfect friends.
- Other kids make fun of me for not joining in.
- I have to maintain good grades.
- I have too much to do.
- My parents fight.
- People don't understand me.
- My peers are angry with me for knowing the answers.

Activity
What causes you stress? What stresses your child?

Why we should teach our children lifeskills

Most children do not know what are appropriate and inappropriate levels of stress. In the present schooling system, our children may not even be taught that they have some control over the stress they face. As they progress through the years, the amount of pressure placed on your child is likely to increase. It is rare that they are taught ahead of time how to deal with all this.

In Singapore especially, we expect our children to be hardworking, driven and ahead of the pack. If they are lag behind their peers, their self-esteem are sometimes bruised by overanxious parents or teachers who believe that they can motivate them by telling them how bad they are. My son came back in tears one day saying, "My teacher told me that my Primary Six exams are 10 times harder than my exams last year. If, after all this studying, I am not still going to pass, why should I bother studying now?" I took him aside and told him that some teachers spur their students by telling them how hard the exams are going to be. And that what his teacher has said is true.

Life in the concrete jungle

Remember the last time you were under extreme stress? Since this could involve any demand or pressure that induced mental and physical tension, an incident should come to mind. You may remember being upset, frightened, excited, annoyed, saddened or surprised.

Stress results from something happening around us or from something happening within. This could be a family crisis, a work problem or a personal difficulty. It can be due to factors as diverse as the ageing of our bodies or the birth of a long-awaited child. The primary effect of stress is to mobilise the body's "fight, flight or fright" system, stimulating the chemical, physical and psychological changes in us to prepare us to cope with a threatening situation.

This system is used when a stressful situation demands action. We can speculate how this system evolved in ancient times. The "fight" impulse could have arose in order to defend one's territory or compete for a mate; "flight" came about when running for one's life from a wild animal or a natural disaster; and "fright" referred to fear when confronted with a wild animal or a natural disaster.

Consider what happens if you come face-to-face with a stressful situation that requires no action. For example, you are late for an important appointment and are held up in a bumper-to-bumper traffic. No movement and no escape. In such a situation, relaxation would be more useful than the biochemical and psychological changes created by the "fight, flight or fright" system.

Hans Selye, the father of modern stress medicine, pointed out in the 1950s that our stress mobilization system is relatively nonspecific. This means that it is mobilized in a similar way to any strong demand, whether short-term or long-term, whether it requires or restricts action, whether it brings good or bad news. Winning a lottery, for example, stresses the body in as much the same way as losing the lottery does. There have been cases of lottery winners dying of a heart attack in their moment of excitement.

Lifeskills development

Bloom's Taxonomy of Cognitive Objectives examines the sequence of developing an increasing mental awareness of stress.

Internalised awareness	5
Pro-active awareness	4
Personal awareness	3
Heightened awareness	2
Undifferentiated awareness of stress	1

1. Undifferentiated awareness of stress

This is the lowest level of understanding—knowing what makes you feel good and bad, how you react to challenging or unpleasant stimuli, and how to keep yourself in your comfort zone. Many people often do not realize their emotional pain or physical discomfort. The pain messages, some of them quite intense, are similar, or not felt at all. Absence of feeling, as in apathy or lethargy, signals denial or suppression that is protecting a person from feeling pain.

2. Heightened awareness

Stress is differentiated into distinct qualities. A person can tell the difference between butterflies in the stomach before an exam and nausea from flu. Coming home alone to an empty house creates a different type of anxiety from doing a public presentation.

3. Personal awareness

A person with personal awareness can describe their personal pattern or cycle of stress in more detail. Sources of stress can be named and stress overload predicted with some accuracy. Such an individual will know that eating a bar of chocolate will give them a headache. They know enough about their bodies and minds to know what will and will not work for them.

4. Pro-active awareness

At this level, individuals shift from passively reacting to stressors to asserting some control over them. Whenever possible, they will eliminate or moderate sources of negative stress within their environment and seek an alternative behaviour that will help them regain strength, energy or peace. These people are unwilling to be seduced by quick fixes. Instead, they are committed to long-term, positive control measures.

5. Internalised awareness

At this highest level, people have a routine. They know what works to keep them healthy, happy and free from stress and they apply this knowledge with enough consistency to reap its benefits. As they keep exploring options using a variation of their lifeskills, they acquire the techniques that will help them cope with emergencies.

Short-term and long-term stress

When a person experiences stress, the immediate action of the nervous system and the endocrine system, the two systems in our bodies that react to stress, is to prepare the body for sustained action. If stress is short-term, there is no problem since the body will have time to rest afterwards, such as when stress comes from a game or preparation for a test. The exhilarating feeling you get is healthy stress, stemming from stimulating activities. This stress can be terminated at will.

However, in the event of long-term stress, which is beyond your conscious control, your body will not have a chance to rest. The effects of this unhealthy stress may begin to show as missed heartbeats, a sense of pounding or even chest pains. Breathing patterns also become more rapid—often the rate is doubled—and shallower, like panting. Under healthy stress, the body adapts itself to the changes. Under unhealthy stress, they create problems. The nose and mouth begin to feel dry from the rapid breathing and chest pains may develop from working the diaphragm muscles so hard. Since signals to breathe come from a buildup of carbon dioxide in the bloodstream, rapid and shallow breathing can create problems: out of breath, dizziness and hyperventilation. This can be easily rectified by breathing into and out of a paper bag. Some psychosomatic effects—physical ailments that arise as a result of emotional instability—of unhealthy stress are more difficult to manage. Decreased rhythmic contractions of the digestive system and vasoconstriction of the gastric glands under stress can produce an upset stomach or constipation. The release of certain hormones can increase stomach acidity and the risk of a gastric ulcer.

Effects of short-term stress

Short-term stress is useful; it gives you the impetus to act and respond effectively to situations. When the stress system is on, many chemical changes occur in the body to prepare you to deal with exciting or challenging events. Learn to recognise them each time they appear. Learning to cope with stress begins with self-awareness. In the short term, the body returns to normal stress level and you remain balanced and healthy. If you notice any of these symptoms continuing in you or your child when the stressful situation is over, you could damage your health.

- furrowed brows
- edginess
- clenched teeth or hands
- wide eyes
- dry mouth
- pale face
- flared nostrils
- faster heartbeat
- biting nails
- cold, sweaty hands or feet
- greater sensitivity to touch
- less sensitivity to pain

Effects of long-term stress

Below are some effects of long-term stress. Prolonged stress is harmful to the body and can lead to a variety of physical disorders.

- appetite loss
- bad skin conditions
- headaches
- backaches
- ulcers and indigestion
- stomach problems
- neck and shoulder tension
- neck aches
- chest tension
- constipation or diarrhoea
- heart problems
- high blood pressure

It also includes the following emotional problems:

- edginess
- withdrawal
- guilt
- aggression
- depression
- worry
- blame
- fear
- boredom
- insomnia
- hyperactivity
- excessive drinking
- drug abuse
- lack of motivation
- anticipatory anxiety

How a person's stress response develops

There are two main ways a stress response develops. In the first, an external stimulus (for example, your teacher yelling at you) leads to physiological arousal (heartbeats faster, face becomes pale), followed by a negative interpretation of arousal ("I must be scared") and a painful emotion (fear). In the second, an external stimulus (such as being late for class) leads to negative thoughts ("My teacher will kill me") and generates physiological arousal (sweaty palms, dry lips and throat, heart beats faster), followed by a painful emotion (anxiety).

How stress is aggravated

When one is stressed, a negative feedback loop is created between the mind and the body. In the first stress response formula, a stressful situation occur. You have butterflies in the stomach and you think, "I must be getting frightened." Your body reacts to the belief that you are becoming fearful by giving you more butterflies in the stomach. Your heart rate speeds up and you get more worked up as the cycle keeps escalating.

Formula two has a similar pattern. You interpret an event as risky by saying to yourself, "This is dangerous. I may get injured." Your body reacts to this thought by some heart pounding and gut wrenching. You interpret this as further cause for concern and think, "This stress is getting way over my head." Your body receives the thought that there is further danger and so escalates its response until you collapse.

How stress is defused

Stress intervention consists of a series of actions. A stress syndrome consists of three factors: your environment, your negative thoughts and your physical responses. By changing any one of the three factors, stress response can be altered, for example, by changing the way you think. Chapter 7 helps you identify distortions in thinking patterns that leads to stress buildup. The exercise below will change the way you respond under stress. By identifying the stress-provoking environment and changing it, the whole stress cycle can be stopped.

STRESS MANAGEMENT TECHNIQUE

Below is a powerful relaxation technique. It consists of two stages. The first stage relaxes the muscles by contracting and releasing them. The second part is a guided visualisation sequence.

Stage A

1. Clench your right hand into a fist and contract it as tightly as you can for five seconds. Relax. Do this three times and contrast how much more relaxed your right hand is compared to your left. Make the comparison only for the first time you do this exercise. Repeat the exercise with your left hand.
2. Contract the muscles of your face, neck and shoulders as tightly as you can for five seconds. Then relax. Repeat three times.
3. Contract the muscles of your stomach and torso as tightly as you can for five seconds. Then relax. Repeat three times.
4. Contract the muscles of your legs and waist as tightly as you can for five seconds. Then relax. Repeat three times.
5. Contract all the muscles in the body as tightly as you can for five seconds. Then relax. Repeat three times.

If, at the end of this process, you are deeply relaxed, carry on to the next stage. If not, go back and repeat steps 1 to 5.

Stage B

For this visualisation exercise, it is best that you have a tape recorded version to listen to. You can make a tape by reading the words very slowly into a tape and then playing it. You can also let your child try it.

"As you lie or sit, become aware of a wave of relaxation moving down your body. As you experience this wave, become aware of the wave moving down from your head down to your forehead. Realise how relaxed and comfortable you feel as the wave continues to move down to the muscles of your jaw. As you become aware of those muscles, become aware of the muscles at the inner corners of your eyes. As you become aware of them, experience the muscles of your eyes becoming limp and you go all the way down...down...down. The wave moves deeper and deeper in you and you feel the wave continue to move down the muscles of your neck. Realise how much deeper you have sunk into— this state of deep comfort and quiet relaxation.

As you realise how relaxed and comfortable you are, feel the wave continue to move down to the muscles of the front and back of your chest. Your eyelids become increasingly heavy now. Heavier than they have ever been and you become aware of the sensations in your body that tell you how deeply you have gone down, in a way that is safe and secure. Know that you are in control of this process, going only as deeply as you wish to continue your many learnings. That's right, it feels really good as the weight on your eyelids keeps increasing and you find yourself more comfortable than you ever thought possible.

Consider how relaxed and comfortable you feel as the wave continues to move down to the muscles of the front and back of your stomach down to your hips. You are sinking to a safe place that you can reach and touch. As you go down...down...down, you can use the sounds in the background to take you down much deeper. Be aware of how relaxed and comfortable you feel as the wave continues to move down to your thigh muscles. The sounds around you now may feel dim. That's alright. You can use them to help you go down much deeper and become more relaxed. Become aware of how heavy the weight of your eyelids are—maybe 5 kg or even 10 kg. Continue to note how relaxed and comfortable you feel as the wave continues to move down to the muscles of your knees, your calves and finally your feet."

Coping with stress

Keep fit

Being fit means your child will be able to handle a large amount of physical and mental stress before he feels the strain. An aerobic activity, such as swimming, running or other sports, would be very useful. Also ensure that he has regular meals and drinks enough water.

Stay cool

In many families, parents and children respond to stress with total denial or by keeping it under wraps. For example, some fathers become verbally or physically abusive or simply withdraw into their quiet shell. Do you keep your cool under stress? This is perhaps one of the most powerful ways of helping your child to cope when he is under stress. If he sees how you work out the important priorities when you are under stress, that is, by doing only what is useful and what is pressing, he is likely to learn this by example. Going for group activities and family outings creates a channel for communication that is outside of the usual channels available to your children. These activities become an anchor that your child can summon at will and use as a resource when he is under stress.

Teaching your child simple ways to cope with stress is crucial. There is no fixed strategy for this; it varies from family to family. Some parents may opt to spend some quiet time together with their child at the end of the day, while others prefer to tackle a problem as soon as it surfaces. Both methods are fine, as long as you and your child review the situation together and work out effective ways of handling it.

Learn to read the environment

A useful skill you could teach your child is to recognise a genuinely friendly person from a potential foe. Many people who lack social skills and adequate judgement share things inappropriately with others. By providing examples and a consistent emotional influence, you would be providing your child with valuable input about relating to people and understanding them better.

Another useful skill is to teach him how to identify when he is feeling distressed or uncomfortable with the level of pressure. Some children are naturally aware that they are under stress and will be upfront in telling you about it. Others may need to be coaxed and persuaded that it is not some personal fault if they experience stress and anxiety.

Managing stressful situations

Let us now look at some common stressful situations and apply the techniques that have been outlined so far. Read out these examples to your child.

- My teachers have impossible expectations.

  As a student, if you are aware that your parents or teachers have unrealistic expectations of you, then you can gently point out their mental distortions. If it is a case of "Jimmy has got higher grades than you", you may wish to tell them that you are not Jimmy. If you are doing the best you can, then they have to accept it.

- My parents expect me to have perfect friends.

  Your parents may be having unrealistic expectations again. It may also be that your friends are not really suitable for you. You may have to make a decision about the type of person you are and the kind of friends you mix with.

- Other kids make fun of me for not joining in.

  Handling peer pressure is one of the hardest things to learn. We all have this herd instinct to want to fit in, be like the others and not stand out. Ask yourself whether you have any cause to regret your decision later if you join them.

- I have too much to do.

  This is a stress situation that all students face. Developing good study habits and effective time management skills will definitely make a major difference.

- My parents fight.

  Your parents may have to get help in resolving their marital conflicts, or it may be necessary for them to seek the help of a teacher or a respected outsider. Above all, remember it is not your fault when your parents fight. Also, be careful not to take sides.

- My peers are angry at me for knowing the answers.

  If you are in any way more capable than your classmates, you are likely to be ahead in your schoolwork. If they are angry at your ability, don't pretend to be dumb. Realise that if you do that, you are only fooling yourself. You would be happier if you are with a group of like-minded friends.

I have designed a questionnaire to help you and your child identify stress points. Go through it carefully with your child.

STRESS POINTS IDENTIFICATION QUESTIONNAIRE
Questions for the parent(s):
1. List five behaviours that you exhibit when you are under stress.
a.
b.
c.
d.
e.
2. What is your predominant style of communication?
3. List five behaviours that your child exhibits when he is under stress.
a.
b.
c.
d.
e.
4. What is his predominant style of communication?

If you have problems answering questions 3 and 4, try communicating with your child. Remember, juvenile deliquency and problems with behaviour begin when communication breaks down between the parent and the child.

Questions for the child:
1. List five behaviours that you exhibit when your are under stress.
a.
b.
c.
d.
e.
2. List five behaviours that your father/mother exhibits when he/she is under stress.
a.
b.
c.
d.
e.

This is an excellent opportunity to discuss these issues and bring the family closer together. As a parent, if you experience difficulty in any part of this exercise, or your child does not feel it appropriate to discuss the above, then it is time to seriously consider your parent-child relationship.

REDUCING STRESS IN RELATIONSHIPS

Go through all these techniques for reducing stress, then help your child go through them.

- Be aware of your own feelings—anger, sadness, rejection, etc. Find a partner and tell the person to say a line that will evoke some emotions in you. Write down what feelings those words evoked. Referring to the strategies mentioned in Chapter 7, discard those feelings. Change a partner and repeat the procedure.
- Avoid exploding, sulking or hiding as a regular means of coping with your life. Identify five areas in your life where you use these inappropriate coping methods.
- Use "I" statements, such as "I think it would be better if...", rather than blaming statements like, "You messed up..."
- Communicate to be heard, not to score points. Identify five occasions in the past when you wanted to win. Then identify five occasions in the past when you wanted to communicate to be heard. What was the difference in your attitude? How did you sound or feel?
- Don't ever assume things about others. (Refer to Chapter 7 about mental distortions). What assumptions have you made about your child or partner that makes you get angry, annoyed and frustrated with their behaviour? Are these assumptions valid?
- Give people your time and respect. How much time do you spend with your family?
- Cooperate with other people. Be a team member both at home and at work. Or are you a one-man show?
- Ask for help and support at home and support others.
- Allow yourself to love and be loved.
- It is not your job to teach the rest of the world right from wrong.
- Talk to someone you trust when you have problems.
- Accept what you cannot change.
- If you are sick, don't pretend that you're not.
- Be realistic about you can achieve.
- Principles are rarely more important than people. Most people can find room for both.
- Don't talk about work after office hours.
- Emphasise your good points.
- Don't take yourself too seriously.
- Balance your work, family and social life.
- Don't be afraid to say "no".
- Use relaxed body language: smile and laugh.

- Make requests and not demands. Requests are flattering and usually fulfilled. Demands challenge others and are often resisted.
- Develop imaginary role-reversal skills. They add empathy and sympathy to relationships. Put yourself in the other person's shoes and help him understand how you see things. You will be less likely to grudge his behaviour if you do.
- Acknowledge that perfection does not exist; compromise and reward yourself for your efforts.
- View yourself through your own eyes. Give yourself permission to relax, speak for yourself and be good to yourself. Know yourself as you are, not what you think you should be.

Chapter 9

LIFESKILLS FOR SUCCESS

Communication patterns
Communication styles:
Passive-style response
Aggressive-style response
Passive-agressive style response
Assertive-style response
Messages from the environment
Assertiveness
Lifeskills for success:
Develop a network of friends
Personal mastery
Creating personal success

Communication patterns

Helping your child to develop appropriate patterns of communication is very important. Communication patterns go beyond mere language patterns of behaviour; they also include body language, knowing how to be at ease in most situations, as well as the ability to bridge cultural gaps and connect with people from different cultures. Such skills are becoming more useful and vital as regional networking increases and entrepreneurs and business leaders need to quickly adapt and be flexible in dealing with different cultural norms in this global village. In future, besides good grades, company executives will be expected to be good team players and communicators.

Communication styles

There are many styles of communication. The major types are the passive, aggressive, passive-aggressive and assertive styles. Children normally learn these styles of behaviour when they observe how the authority figures in their lives communicate with others.

Passive-style response

People with this style allow others to make the decisions and control their feelings or actions. Such individuals may not even be aware that their thoughts and feelings matter. They often deny their own feelings and consistently put others' needs before their own. They also work very hard at pleasing others. These people tend to be drawn to aggressive people who will, however, put them down. This leaves them hurt, angry, let down and depressed because they do not know how to get others to meet their needs. Passive people often develop arthritis and cancer.

Some people are passive because they never learnt other styles of communication. They may have come from a family background where any attempt at assertive behaviour was put down by looks of disapproval from their parents. They may think that the only way to keep the peace and avoid conflict is to be a doormat.

Passive people may also equate being assertive with aggression. Within the Asian context, being passive, for women, is often mistaken to be feminine and culturally appropriate. Some of these women may not even know that they have the right to stand up for themselves. In some societies, women get praised for being passive and amenable. Some of them may not even be able to handle the responsibility of being in charge of their lives.

Aggressive-style response

Someone operating with an aggressive-style response is likely to be loud, abusive, pushy and sarcastic. These individuals gossip, boss, tease or publicly humiliate others or even threaten others. They are not at all guilty about achieving their goals at the expense of others since they feel that their own needs should come first. While an aggressive style makes the person feel powerful on the surface, it leaves him with very few friends and many unfulfilled needs. These people are often not trusted or respected by others.

People who are aggressive behave this way because they may not know other ways of being assertive, or they may mistake aggression for assertiveness. They feel that if they are not intimidating to others, they will be perceived as weak and losing control.

These people have a need to dominate and win all the time. They may never learn how to compromise, share and support others. They are often rewarded for their aggression by being placed in positions where they can be more aggressive. They often do not know how to be responsible and responsive to others. These people often develop high blood pressure and heart conditions.

Passive-aggressive style response

Those who operate with this style have traits of the above two styles. They do not overtly dominate or abuse other people but seek control or revenge covertly. Passive-aggressive people often say "yes" insincerely.

They also tend to be persistently late and rarely do they follow through their commitments—something vital is always left undone. They keep quiet when an unfair or difficult decision is made and then quietly sabotage it behind the scenes. Passive-aggressive people never really learn how to express their anger and they often fear the anger and disapproval of authority figures. Like passive people, they see themselves as victims who cannot do anything about the situation they are in.

Some individuals are passive-aggressive because this is the only type of response they can generate. They feel angry but often feel guilty about being angry. These people may have come from a punitive background where they were punished for expressing their feelings openly when they were young. They may feel that they are not important enough unless they can stir up an issue. They may resent people in power but are afraid of shouldering responsibility and asserting power themselves. These people often develop allergies and respiratory problems.

Assertive-style response

Assertive behaviour means that you can stand up for yourself and act in your own best interest without undue anxiety. You can comfortably and honestly express your feelings or exercise your rights without denying others of theirs. Examples of assertive-style responses include talking to a teacher when confused, seeking a friend's help about an assignment, rejecting drugs or alcohol and defending yourself against unfair criticism.

An assertive person is capable of being honest. He can take constructive criticism positively and will respect the rights of others in the way he expects the very same rights from others. He is unlikely to deliberately hurt others emotionally or physically. Nor would he lie to gain control over a situation.

Activity

Discuss with your child the assertive-style behaviours he requires in his life. If he does not possess these skills, refer to Chapter 11 for behaviour modification techniques to learn these behaviours.

Messages from the environment

Children are constantly being bombarded with messages from the environment. Each of these messages advocate a certain code of behaviour or feeling, telling them what is appropriate in a particular situation. In many television shows, women are often misleadingly portrayed as weak, passive and dependant on the strong, macho men in their lives. Strong women are portrayed as vamps, or a heroine in a diabolically cunning plot or a successful woman who has everything except a man in her life.

What types of message do you give your child? Is there a discrepancy between your behaviour and your words? If you say, "All humans are created equal," and demonstrate racial prejudice and male chauvinism, you have just taught your child another character trait—hypocrisy.

Assertiveness

Being assertive means standing up for your rights and beliefs. As your child begins to assert his rights, he will become more confident. He will feel that he is on par with his peers. Being assertive also demands that your child means what he says and says what he means. His demeanour will attract like-minded friends who are equally assertive and honest. When your child remains calm in frantic situations, it is another form of assertive behaviour. Such an individual feels a sense of control over their destiny. As a result, they experience less anxiety. Some parents may agree to these ideas on the surface, but when their child speaks up for his rights, they try to undermine his confidence. As a parent, here are some things you can do to help your child develop assertiveness.

- Draw clear rules for communication in the family.
- Clearly outline a list of duties for everyone. Penalties should be clearly spelled out. This may be pasted on the refrigerator. The duties and penalties should be determined by group consensus.
- When your child is speaking, listen to him at his level. Do not judge him as an adult or scold him for his immature thinking. This may seem elementary but when I was studying martial arts, my instructor

told me a story. A very young boy once joined his class. A couple of months later, after a practice, my instructor saw the boy's father scold him for being uncoordinated in his practice. The instructor took the father aside and asked him, "How long did it take you to become good at a sport? Don't you realise that at his age, he doesn't have the motor skills to move as swiftly as the older children?"

- While some families gather once a week to talk about things that happened to them for the past seven days, other families benefit from a more carefully planned procedure. My family is one of them. My wife and I came up with the following rules for our weekly session when our increasingly verbal son made it more and more ineffective.
  - Everyone has five minutes to talk while the others listen.
  - After listening, the others may comment on what they have heard.
  - If the listeners are in doubt about the purpose of the communication, they can clarify with the speaker.

Since we did not want to blame anyone but felt that grievances had to be voiced, we decided that comments about undesirable behaviour should start with, "I felt Y when you did X . What was your intent in doing X?" The other person is then given an opportunity to explain.

Once you and your child start communicating like this, you will become aware of the times when you are blaming others. When you listen to the explanations given, you become aware of the other person's thinking pattern. The above procedure also helps children learn a new way of communication.

Lifeskills for success
Develop a network of friends

Teaching your child the skills to develop a network of friends will often stand him in good stead with the passage of years. This will provide him an opportunity to practice his social interaction skills. He will learn to mingle with different individuals. These skills will come in handy when he starts working.

Personal mastery

Throughout the book, I have discussed the emotional and mental skills crucial for success in life. This section outlines a macro-strategy for lifelong success. I have left this most significant and crucial part to the last because it is based on many of the other skills. Also, we can only suitably appreciate this macro-strategy when we have looked at the overall picture of what it takes to succeed. Personal mastery consists of:

1. **Metacognition**
   Also known as raising consciousness among the general populace, metacognition refers to the ability to examine the nature of life and identify what really matters. In the Buddhist tradition, this has been referred to as mindfulness. By being mindful, you or your child can decide what you want in life and then work out a suitable course of action. As you gain an insight into yourself, you can better understand your needs and wants and devise suitable ways of realising them.

2. **Using imagery**
   One of the most dramatic uses of imagery was by Olympic athletes who vividly imagined engaging in their sport before they physically did it. Olympic ski racers used to mentally traverse the route they were going to take in their mind's eye before actually doing it. This practice dramatically improved their performance.

3. **Framing and re-framing events**
   Research has shown that it is not what happens that matters as much as the significance we tag to these events. By generating multiple meanings to events, the possibility of coming up with a creative explanation for that event becomes greater. A useful interpretation of an event will allow you to delve more deeply into your creative aspects and come up with more fruitful endeavours. For example, if your child did badly in a Maths test and decides that he is stupid and

129

cannot study Maths, he will then give up. If he decides, however, that he did badly because he did not understand the key concepts, then that could motivate him to study differently and get good grades.

4. **Integrating new perspectives**

Brain research has shown that our view of the world is physiologically limited by our genetics and life experiences. By incorporating the perspectives of others, we expand our innate life experiences. By noticing when someone interprets something differently from you, you are given an opportunity to look at life from a different angle.

When your child plans for his career, he may think in terms of a single career. But what is most likely to happen is that he will undergo several career changes either as a developmental sequence, that is, from student to undergraduate to fresh on the job to senior executive to manager, or when he moves from one job to another. How well he can envision the different possibilities will be very useful for him.

Creating personal success

We all need to feel that we are successful by the standards we set ourselves. Having unclear expectations and goals can set one up for a lifetime of failure. Someone who feels he has succeeded possesses immense physical, emotional or financial resources that he can draw upon. On the other hand, when an individual thinks he has not succeeded, he may feel that he is heading nowhere and may be filled with a sense of despair.

Activity

Below are situations that you can discuss with your child. Ask yourself in each situation, what is your preferred mode of response? What about your child's? If the situations below are not relevant to you, explore the emotions they evoke in you.

1. Your child has failed to do his homework for a week. His teacher wants an explanation. How do you handle it?
2. Your child has been found to be picking on children younger than him. What do you do?

Chapter 10

GENERATING NEW
BEHAVIOUR

How we store memories
Anchoring
Controlling your emotional states
Getting along with others
Matching body language
Taking note of what matters
Goal setting model
Turning your dreams into reality
Walking a mile in another's shoe
Cost-benefit analysis

How we store memories

Nearly every event has a visual, auditory, kinaesthetic, olfactory and gustatory component, thus we normally use all of our senses to absorb the information. Thanks to the work of Richard Badler and John Grinder, the founders of Neuro-Linguistic Programming (NLP), we now know that our memories are coded in a similar fashion. They also discovered that it is not an event that produces a particular emotion for us but the meaning we assign or attach to that event.

Further research done by Badler and Grinder has shown that by changing the way a piece of information has been stored in our memory, we can often change the meaning that we have assigned to that memory. When someone says they have an unpleasant memory or an uncomfortable experience, they are actually referring to the meaning and emotions they have assigned to that experience. The brain's way of coding information is so precise that the moment you change the way that memory is stored in the brain, that experience is no longer stored and interpreted in the same way. Some of you may remember having an unpleasant childhood experience. As you grow older, the memory of that experience changes and now you may even laugh at the incident you had formerly considered traumatic.

Most people simply let their brains randomly show them any picture and then they proceed to feel good or bad as the case may be. Have you ever thought it possible to intentionally vary the brightness of an internal image in order to feel different? It has been said that time can heal all wounds, but with the following technique, you can change the feelings you associate with your memories without having to wait for years. Think of a past experience that was very pleasant—one you have not thought of for a long time. Pause for a moment to go back to that memory and be sure that you can see what you saw at the time the event occurred. You may want to close your eyes to see it more clearly.

As you recall the memory, change the brightness of the image and notice how your feelings change in response. First, make the image brighter and brighter. Then make it dimmer and dimmer until you can barely see it. Increasing brightness usually increases the intensity of the feelings and decreasing brightness usually decreases the intensity.

Now think of an unpleasant memory, something that makes you feel unhappy. Slowly make the image dimmer and dimmer. If you turn the brightness down far enough, the event won't bother you any more. There are, however, some exceptions. If you make a picture so bright that it washes out the details and becomes almost white, that will reduce, rather than increase, the intensity of your feelings. For some people, the correlation is reversed in most contexts: increasing brightness decreases the intensity of their feelings.

Brightness is only one of the many elements you can vary. Now pick another pleasant memory and vary the size of that picture. Make it bigger and bigger, then smaller and smaller. Notice how your feelings intensify and fade correspondingly. There are again exceptions to this pattern. When the picture becomes too large, it may seem ridiculous or unreal. If making an unpleasant experience extremely big turns it into a ridiculous and laughable memory, then you can use this method to make yourself feel better. Find out what works for you so that you can learn to control your experience.

If you think about it, it is not surprising why brightness and size should affect your feelings about an event. People talk about "a dim future" or "bright prospects", or say things like, "Everything looks black" and "My mind went blank." These phrases are usually not metaphorical but a precise description of what the person is experiencing. If you want to learn how your brain works, take any experience and try changing each of the visual elements: colour, distance, depth, duration, clarity, scope, speed. Do the same thing you did with brightness and size, go in one direction and then the other to see how it changes your experience. Remember to change only one element at a time. If not, you will not know which one or by how much each one is affecting your experience. I would also suggest that you start with a pleasant experience.

Anchoring

An anchor is a signal to your neurology to change its state. Anchors are often unconscious. You may hear the national anthem and feel the desire to stand at attention, or hear someone who sounds like a teacher you dislike and thus move away from him. Some people smell balachan (spicy, fermented prawn paste) and recall their grandmother's cooking.

Controlling your emotional states

Optimal state setting

- Remember a time when you felt relaxed, comfortable and alert. Make this experience a multisensory one with colour, pictures and sound.
- Experience a wave travelling from the top of your head down your body. When it moves down your forehead, release the tightness in the inner corners of your eyes and the tension in your jaws.
- Deepen this state by repeating the process for about three times.
- Set a trigger for this state by putting a finger and thumb together at the height of the process.

The above technique is really useful when children are introduced to a potentially stressful situation such as the first day at school. My son used to be scared of going to school. Instead of setting an anchor for relaxation, my wife and I set another anchor for him: being "Superman". Whenever he encountered a scary scenario, he was to activate this anchor. That was the last we saw of the problem.

OPTIMAL STATE SETTING

Creating positive anchors for your child
- Recall a picture of a time when he felt good.
- Turn up the brightness, volume and size of the image.
- Find out what makes the picture powerful and inspiring for him.
- Anchor the state by touching his index finger with his thumb.

Wiping out the bad feelings: create an anchor for comfort.
- Make a picture of the unpleasant event.

- Select an inappropriate soundtrack to play along with the picture (preferably a funny one).
- Give the picture a new frame.
- Now, play the music with the newly framed picture.
  How does your child feel? If he has the elements right, the unpleasant event will become neutral or insignificant. This technique helps to wipe out fears and anxieties. Children who are scared or anxious about school, tuition or a particular teacher will find this exercise useful.

Modelling new behaviour

- Identify a time when he felt a particular situation seems more than he could handle. Put the situation aside.
- Create a sphere about himself and remember a time when he felt powerful, strong, excited and enthusiastic. Explore fully what he feels, hears, sees and the messages he is telling himself. Have him put the image in his lower right hand side of his mind. (See Position A below.)
- While standing in the sphere, recall someone whom he respects and admires. He then watches him cope resourcefully with the situation that he cannot deal with. Explore fully what he thinks, feels, hears, sees and the messages the person is telling him. Which of their qualities is he currently using in his life? Which of their qualities can he learn to use with ease now? Put this picture in the upper left hand side of his mind. (Position B)
- Recall a time when he acted resourcefully and powerfully in a situation. Explore fully what he feels, hears, sees and the messages he is telling himself. Check and see if this resource is powerful enough for him. Put this picture in the lower left hand side of his mind. (Position C)
- Take a look at how he would now respond to the original situation if he had all of the different strengths built in. See his behaviour as it occurs outside his sphere. He can keep changing what he sees happening until it looks and sounds right. Then leaving his sphere of influence, he can step into the picture and test if it feels right. When it does, he steps back into his sphere of influence. Put this picture in the upper right hand side of his mind. (Position D)

B	D
C	A

- Roll his eyes gently and slowly as he experiences all of these four states. After he has done it a few times, clockwise and anticlockwise, have him recall the original situation. If he has done this correctly, he will feel that he has more than enough resources to cope with the situation. He will become aware of how else he can behave in future with his new skills and resources and can actually mentally rehearse these new behaviours.

I once worked with a young man, David. He had been a national ski champion and an army officer and was working as a ski instructor when suddenly, he stopped eating properly, gave up his job and kept running away from home. After consulting psychiatrists and physicians to no avail, David's girlfriend brought him in to see us.

When I talked to David, I was struck by his sense of responsibility and accountability. His parents were separated and I suspected, at some level, he still blamed himself for it. David also had unrealistic expectations of himself and the burden of these beliefs overwhelmed him. He kept telling himself, "I am not good enough", "I do not know enough" and "I will never learn to get all these new things right."

I began helping him by first improving his nutritional status with suitable supplements. Then I took him through the above exercise. I made him recall the times when he had felt powerful, excited and enthusiastic, when he won trophies during his water skiing competitions (A). Then I had him recollect someone he admired and respected for his resourcefulness in coping with situations he could not handle; in David's case, it was his father (B). He went on to picture the best wins of his life in a series of powerful events and crystallised this image (C). Next, he imagined what it would be like if he did all that he had to do with these skills (D). I made him create a movie of himself doing different things. He kept altering these pictures until he felt comfortable. Then he stepped in and out of this movie and kept changing it until it felt right. After five one-hour visits over five weeks, David called to say he was too busy to see me. When he finally visited me a month later, he told me he had been busy training to defend his skiing title and that he had been accepted into the Air Force as a candidate for pilot training. Most importantly, he was brimming with confidence and vitality.

Getting along with others

Some young people have a knack for getting along with others. They step into a group and within minutes they are accepted into the group.

Others never really get along with others. Perhaps the easiest way of explaining how your child can learn to get along with other children is to place him with a cat. A child who is good at interpreting nonverbal communication will know after some interaction what the cat likes and dislikes and how it wants to be approached. This is especially important as your child will meet more and more people as he grows older and steps into society. As he moves up the hierarchy, he will find that an inability to communicate with others will impede his progress.

Just as the cat likes it when your child makes meowing sounds, people get comfortable when someone they meet for the first time adopts familiar ways of relating to them. This involves everything from walking and talking a similar fashion to using similar words. Imitation is often the most sincere form of flattery.

Matching body language

Children who are adept in reading people's body language often end up duplicating the physical posture of the person they are with. Very young children are often the best imitators of body language because they mimic the behaviour of their parents and other authority figures before they begin to learn the nuances of behaviour.

Teaching your child this ability will equip him with an invaluable asset. He can go anywhere in the world and feel at home. There are a number of ways this can be done. When your child is with a friend and he keeps doing exactly what his friend is doing, like nodding his head to the right the same way his friend is doing it, he is matching him. If he nods his head to the right in a similar fashion while his friend is doing it to the left, he is mirroring him. If he decides to move his foot in rhythm to his friend's head nods, this is called cross mirroring.

When I was a student , I have a friend who was superb at public relations. He got along so well that he could be accepted by different groups of students who disliked one another. When he was with someone, he often listened sympathetically and made the person feel that he was really understood. If he made a suggestion, he would make sure there was a deep sense of connection before doing so. Not surprisingly, most people would go along with his suggestions.

The next part of communication involves building rapport. To connect with someone, take about your similar hobbies, pastimes or play games that you both know. Talking about the other person's areas of interest is another good way of building rapport with that person.

Activity

1. When your child goes to school, he can:
a. On the first day, match a friend's behaviour for three minutes.
b. On the second day, mirror another friend's behaviour for three minutes.
c. On the third day, cross mirror another friend's behaviour for three minutes. Have him report to you what this experience was like.
2. On the fourth day, tell him to persuade his friends about something. This time though, he has to get into conversation with his friend and:
a. Mismatch his friend (make sure he does not do anything similar at all) and then persuade him for three minutes. What happens? How did he feel?
b. He then enters into rapport with him and persuades. Does he notice anything happening? Ask him if he found it easier to persuade them to his point of view when he did this.

Taking note of what matters

In order to match his friends, your child needs to observe what his friends do and attach meanings to their behaviours. If your child did the previous activity properly, he should be able to note different responses from his friends. You should also point out to him that the responses that really matter are the ones that his friends do not say.

When you are talking to someone, do you listen to what they say, or are you busy telling yourself stories inside your head? Any data that you receive has to fitted into a context before it becomes information. So when you communicate with someone, you need to be aware what that person's posture or gesture means. Children who are adept at these skills are able to observe someone's breathing patterns and work out whether they are relaxed or tense. They are sensitive to facial expressions and gestures and are able to figure out pretty well what they show. Children who are effective communicators often evaluate how their communication is being received. They will keep changing their methods of sending a message until it finally gets through. Those who have an unsafe home environment often have more difficulty with communication because when their parents get angry, they are in for some physical or emotional abuse. So a caring and safe environment is an essential prerequisite for these skills to develop.

Activity

Discuss with your child the meaning of each facial expression that your child makes. Ask him what he thinks of the different moods you are in. What labels does he attach to them? Ask if your child knows the best time to ask you for something. You will be surprised at what you will learn.

Goal setting model

For many people, goal setting turns out to be an exercise in futility because they lack the skills to set achievable goals. To set a goal, the following guidelines have to be adhered to. If you stick firmly to them, you will always reach your goal.

Steps to achieving goals

- Definition

  Be as specific as possible in defining your objective. Include all elements that might be involved. If your child wants to improve his grades for Mathematics, set a specific grade like A or B.
- Purpose

  Why do you want to achieve this particular goal? What will achieving the goal do for you? If you set a goal for your child, you are setting him up for failure. Your child needs a compelling reason to achieve his goal, thus it has to be something he wants to achieve. It could be something as simple as improving his mathematics grade.

- Information needed to achieve the goal

  What do you need to know to accomplish this goal? Try to anticipate all the information you need, then apply the skills you know to gather the information.

- Resources

  What strengths do you have that will enable you to accomplish the goal? How can you best utilize them? What strengths does your child have that would help him in this goal?

- Roadblocks

  What might prevent you from accomplishing your goal? How can you clear these obstacles? Does your child get very upset when his grades are poor? If he does, teach him ways to control his emotions.

- Steps

  How will you go about accomplishing your goal? List each possible step and include the date that you will accomplish it. Help your child draw up a timetable to study the individual topics and set a definite time limit on achieving it.

- Other important issues pertaining to the goal

  What else can you think of that is important to achieving this goal? If your child has an unsympathetic mathematics teacher, you can teach him ways to cope with his teacher.

Turning your dreams into reality

Have you watched Walt Disney's cartoons? Do you know why he is so successful? One of Walt Disney's unique characteristics is his ability to explore an issue from a number of different perceptual positions. Disney is a dreamer, realist and critic, all rolled into one. This, in essence, is the structure of creativity. Creativity without any of the three aspects does not get fully realised.

Disney is not just a creative dreamer, he is also very skilled at making those dreams come true. He is committed to seeing visually whatever story he is developing. His primary strategy and major strength as a realist is to break his dreams into a sequence of manageable chunks. Then he will produce a set of still drawings that represent the chronological sequence of critical events in his story so that anyone who picks up his drawings can easily follow the story outline. After the critical chunks have been defined, the individual drawings connecting these pictorial milestones are filled in by the secondary animation team.

Disney's animation is special because of his ability to step into the shoes of his characters, take on their character and see the world through their eyes. As a result, he can intimately experience his imaginary character's motives and behaviour. This practice also allows him to experience how his characters may act in a particular situation rather than use reasoning to predict his characters' actions. This role playing is a critical aspect of his ability as a realist. He is able to make his story tangible for others who could then concretely experience his dream.

The last phase of Disney's creative structure was the most painful. As a critic, he has to evaluate the fruit of his labour. So his focus shifts from spontaneous creativity and organised exploration to a critical evaluation of the finished product.

Activity

Use Walt Disney's strategy to help your child draw up a chart of his goals.

Walking a mile in another's shoe

Mahatma Gandhi once wrote that, in preparation for a meeting, he would consider an issue through the eyes of a Hindu, a Muslim and a Briton. He would think of the actual people that he believed represented these points of view and then step into their positions to truly understand their opinions. Gandhi would also consider his negotiation outcomes through the eyes of the world, from an observer perspective, before proposing them. Since he had adopted all the different perspectives, he was often able to predict all the possible outcomes, contributing significantly to his great vision and profound wisdom.

WALKING A MILE IN ANOTHER'S SHOES

Pick a situation which involves two or more people. Then assume the role of each person and go through all the possible lines they might say. Let your child watch you go through this process. Below is an example of a situation that you can use. Remember, in the incident below, you are playing all the different roles. This means that, in the actual situation, you would have all the possibilities and permutations covered and mapped out like Gandhi did. This is a useful procedure for your child to learn, whether he has to take part in a debate or persuade his teacher or friends about something.

Example

You want to suggest to your director that the company needs to install a comprehensive staff welfare programme. You will be discussing this with the managing director, Mr Woo, and the director of human resource department, Mr Lee. So it might be useful to have three chairs each representing the different people. When you sit down in each chair, try to assume the mannerisms of the people involved in order to gain a greater insight into their thinking process.

You : Gentleman, I like to suggest something that will increase our company's productivity, reduce staff turnover and in the long term, increase our profits.

Woo: Sounds good. What is it going to cost us?

Lee : Seems like an area for the other departments, can you tell me why am I needed here?

You : Because this falls into your department sir.

Lee : (suspiciously) What do you mean?

You : Do you remember I was sent to Germany last year to study a stress management programme? There was some interest about how we could tailor it to our company. This is what the meeting is all about.

Woo: Did the programme work? Do they have statistics and figures to prove its success?

You : Most companies who implemented this programme reduced their health care costs by 15% and reduced staff turnover by 12%. Productivity on the average increased by 14.5%.

Woo: That sounds impressive. I would like you and Mr Lee to draft a preliminary proposal.

Now let your child go through this process with a situation on hand.

Cost-benefit analysis

What you link pain and pleasure to shapes your destiny. The problem with most of us is, we tend to focus on avoiding pain and gaining pleasure in the short run. This may result in suffering years down the road, e.g., people who smoke run a high risk of contracting cancer. To succeed while preserving the things we value, we have to be able to suffer short-term pain in order to reap long-term pleasure. You must be able to put aside the passing moments of terror or temptation and focus on what's most important in the long term—your values and personal goals.

COST-BENEFIT ANALYSIS

1. Write down four actions that you have been putting off but will commit to doing from now on.
2. Under each action, write down why you have not taken action. In the past, what pain have you linked to performing this action?
3. Note down all the pleasures you have had in the past by indulging in this negative pattern.
4. If you don't change now, what will it cost you? What is it going to cost you in the next six months, two years, three, four five years? What is it going to cost you emotionally? What is it going to cost in terms of your self-image? Or energy level? Or relationships with the people you care about most? How does that make you feel?
5. Do a cost-benefit analysis of changing the behaviour now.
6. What is the pleasure that you will receive by taking each of these actions right now? Make a long list to give yourself an emotional high.
7. Now do this exercise with your child.

Example

Let's imagine that your child has not doing his Chinese homework because he finds the work too difficult. We will look at how the six questions will help lay out the parameters.

1. He commits to attend tuition classes regularly so that it will help him catch up. He also commits to watching more Chinese movies. He will speak to you or his grandparents in Mandarin.
2. His past experiences in doing Chinese homework was painful and difficult. Avoiding it meant relief.
3. He could do other things like playing computer games in his spare time. You can set up a rule that he can only play computer games after he has done his Chinese homework for the day.

4. He can expect his Chinese to deteriorate as the years go by. He will encounter increasing difficulty communicating with those who use this language. He may not be able to study the other subjects he likes in upper secondary because he is not eligible for the right classes.

5. Do a cost-benefit analysis if he changes the behaviour.

Costs	Benefits
Has to work at improving his Chinese	Schoolwork becomes manageable
	Gets good grades
Has to do extra tuition	Will get teacher's approval

6. Schoolwork becomes manageable.
   Can expect to get better grades.
   Can expect to get on better with his Chinese teacher.
   Higher chance of going to the right classes.
   Can make exciting pictures of the above to get himself motivated to make these changes.

Chapter 11
EDUCATION

Education is for life
There are ups and downs in studying
Learn how and where to find information
Finish what you start
It's better to ask stupid questions than be stupid
Learn while you are young
Satisfy the examiners but learn for yourself
The ideal education system:
Don't judge or limit our children
Teachers are not educators or punishers
Teach the systems approach
Teach the principle of abundance
Use innovative teaching methods
Learn by exploring options
Learn from games and role-play
Let children learn what they like
Encourage lifelong learning

If your children ask you what school is about, here are some insights I drew from my own experiences as a student and a teacher.

Education is for life

Going to school is the start of one's education. There are many valuable skills to learn in school. Never mistake what your child learns there to be the only education he is going to have. He can always learn from people around him, anywhere, any time. There are no limits to learning.

There are ups and downs in studying

In the present education system, academic results are what people judge you by. No matter what people say, grades do count. Tell your child to study hard so that he will not regret it 10 years from now. However, while studying, he must be fair and compassionate. Practice a little humility and help his peers when he is ahead. If he is ranked lower than desired, you should not worry excessively. He will have another chance.

Learn how and where to find information

My wife, Ai Mee, who trained in Australia as a librarian, said she was forever grateful for her training because she learned then how to do research. That is one of the gifts a formal education can provide you. Teach your child how to make effective use of libraries, reference sources, the Internet and CD-Roms to gather information. One effective way to cultivate your child's interest in doing research is, instead of telling your child why the sky is blue when he asks you, look it up in the encyclopedia and read the answer to him. That way, he will understand that he too can find answers from books.

Activity

Give your child a project to research on using the library, Internet and other sources of information. Ask him how he feels about doing research.

Finish what you start

Edison's definition of genius was 1% inspiration and 99% perspiration. Perspiration means hard work. Many school projects require perseverance. Your child should finish what he starts. Once this attitude is imprinted in him, whenever problems crop up, his "never-say-die" attitude will be awakened and he will not admit defeat even before trying. If your child copes with difficulties by saying, "This is too difficult," and gives up trying, then the same attitude will manifest itself in other areas of his life. It will be hard for him to attain success then.

Better to ask stupid questions than be stupid

Our school system penalises us for making mistakes. Being afraid of making mistakes is the most fatal and paralysing habit you can develop. Every major scientific discovery had been preceded by hundreds, if not thousands, of mistakes. Being able to ask questions to clarify your understanding is crucial to intellectual growth and understanding. If your child's teacher scolds him for asking questions or does not answer him, that is a sign of the teacher's inability, not your child's.

Activity

When your child asks you a question, give him feedback on what is a good question and why.

Learn while you're young

The time to make mistakes and maximise learning is when you are young. Encourage your child to explore and acquire as many skills as possible in his free time. I came from a family where I was not encouraged to explore and learn things beyond the realm of my parents' imagination. But I went ahead with many activities anyway while staying within safety limits. I experimented with drama, martial arts, sports, creative writing and a wide range of meditative experiences. This is why I now have a reservoir of experiences to draw upon.

Activity

What are you doing to ensure that your child is exposed to drama, music, sports, writing and other experiences?

Satisfy the examiners but learn for yourself

Since your child's ability is judged by how well he does in school, you may want to use all the skills outlined in my previous book *Awakening the Genius in Your Child* to help him achieve good grades. Remind your child that he should learn for himself, not for the sake of passing his exams. What he can do is, for an open-ended question, find the answers that will satisfy the examiners and then figure out three other ways of answering the same question that would satisfy him.

Activity

Examine your child's academic skills. If you have problems, refer to *Awakening the Genius in Your Child*.

The ideal education system
Don't judge or limit our children

Our education system assumes that all children are equal in ability and that they are equally ready to learn a topic at the same time. Those who learn something faster than normal are placed in the better classes while those who cannot learn at the class' speed or methodology are considered slow and inferior. Many people still believe that those who do well in class are intellectually able and the others who don't do as well are dumb.

Our education system has produced a large pool of well-trained technocrats but not enough entrepreneurs with the gungho to venture overseas to set up new businesses. Few people dare take risks or grab opportunities to strike out on their own. One needs to have critical thinking skills to be able to take calculated risks and make good use of opportunities. To foster our children's entrepreneurial spirit, we should allow them to initiate their own projects and encourage their creativity.

Teachers are not educators and punishers

Robert T. Kiyosaki, in his fascinating book *Do You Have To Go To School To Be Rich And Happy*, proposed that students should study in groups. All the group members would then receive the same grade, which is the average of all their results. He argued that this way, the smarter students would be committed to improving the grades of the less able ones.

In such a system, teachers are facilitators rather than punishers. There will be a contractual agreement between the student, his parents, the teacher and the class as a whole. The contract would stipulate that the student has to be committed to his studies, attend all classes, be punctual and do the assigned homework. Parents would supervise compliance of the child's contract as well as attend parent-teacher meetings, fund-raising activities for the school and other events necessary for the successful operation of the school. The teacher would do whatever it takes to help the child advance to the next level. Such a system would foster a strong team spirit, cooperation and result in a win-win situation. Misery and loneliness would decrease because when one student is doing badly, the others would help him improve his grades. If one child's parents are not able to provide support to their child, all the other parents would help this child because they don't want their children's grades to suffer.

Teach the systems approach

To use the systems approach in teaching would be to provide students with the framework of a subject and its applications rather teaching it in bits and pieces. For example, students could embark on a farm project and learn biology. One of the reasons why those trained in mathematics, physics or engineering could adapt to areas outside of their expertise was their training. Children taught using an overview approach rather than a piecemeal approach would develop the ability to look at underlying patterns in the world about them and come to insightful conclusions quickly. The field of medicine is going to be radically transformed by students who are taught this way.

Teach the principle of abundance

Most children feel that their future financial ability is limited because of their poor academic performance. This is wrong. If children are taught the principle of abundance or resource reallocation in their lives, they would never lack anything. The idea of scarcity is a mindset that can be overcome. Thanks to advances in transportation technology, resources would never be scarce if there is a concerted effort at their reallocation, e.g., tons of foods grown in farms that are otherwise dumped in the ocean to control prices and serve political needs could be offered to poorer countries, who would appreciate the aid very much.

Use innovative teaching methods

Research has shown that innovative teaching methodology can improve the efficiency of learning by as much as 300%. One of the most powerful methods for use in teaching is using music in learning, for example, baroque music is useful in improving memory and retention. Using different colours to represent information and mind maps to convey and collate information increases one's learning ability.

The highly structured, rigid teaching methods of present schools tend to break everything down into its elements. Only a few people will excel in such an environment. Most children learn only when topics are taught and applied in an appropriate context. For example, using mental sums when buying sweets.

At this point, you may find my comments too idealistic, but let me tell you what my son's primary five English teacher once said, "I only have them (the students) for a year, so I must make use of this precious opportunity to maximise their learning and growing." Her classes are fun-filled experiences. She would use stories to explain her lessons and students were encouraged to role play before writing compositions. She did not believe in making them do too much written work, allowing them to be creative rather than be bound by rules. My son loved her class and the grades of the class were way above average.

Contrast this with his primary six class teacher. She screamed at them for not doing their work, penalise them for not bringing their books, terrorise them by telling them that PSLE is going to be ten times harder than their school examinations. If you treat your children like idiots, they will definitely live down to your expectations. This is the Pygmillion effect. In an experiment, a group of students with below average grades were told that they were gifted, while another group with above average grades were told that they were normal. After six months, the first group performed like gifted students while the second group had average results. So do you want to treat your child like an idiot or a genius?

Learn by exploring options

Give your child a chance to try out different occupations by going for several apprenticeships. Arrange this during his school holidays. In some cases, it may even be necessary to take an extended leave from school if you think it will help him decide on what he wants. Sometimes your child may feel that he does not need to go to school because he can always get a job at McDonald's. Tell him that if he wants to be independent, he has to go all out: earn his own living, pay for his food and lodging and move out of your house. He is only allowed to take his clothes, not the CD player or the video player. Most young people faced with the option of having to make their own living wake up in a hurry to the benefits of living at home with all their expenses paid.

Activity

Encourage your child to try out a different job during his vacation.

Learn from games and role-play

Kinaesthetic activities can enable us to remember and lock in a lesson. Games and role-playing are very effective ways of teaching subjects such as science. Having a student whirl a pail of water without wetting himself will teach him the principle of centrifugal and centripetal forces.

Let children learn what they like

When we are interested in what we are learning, maximal retention occurs. In Calvin and Hobbes, Calvin's father once expressed concern over Calvin's grades. He said to Calvin, "But you like learning and reading, don't you? What happened in school?" Calvin's answer was short and to the point. "We don't learn about dinosaurs." If the school had taught about dinosaurs, Calvin would be a grade A student.

Activity

Identify one subject area that your child is fascinated in and encourage his exploration.

Encourage lifelong learning

Many people have realised continuous learning is essential to stay ahead, not just to maintain the standard of living. If your child specialises too early and limits his own learning, he may not be able to find the niche that best suits him. However, even if he has found his niche, he still has to constantly upgrade his skills.

When I first started my practice, I thought my years in formal study would be enough. But all they prepared me for was to be a good naturopathic physician. I had to learn through the painful process of trial and error how to be a good accountant, financial planner, marketing consultant and product promoter before my practice picked up.

The job market is becoming more competitive. Employers are demanding more from their staff. They want team players because we are moving out of one-man operations into a corporate world. As we increase our interactions with regional economies, we need leaders and entrepreneurs equipped with these skills to live, learn and flourish. These leaders will be your children.

Chapter 12

LIFESKILLS FOR PARENTS AND TEACHERS

Rapport
Rapport and motivation
Connecting with others
Ways of connecting nonverbally
Calibration
Sensory acuity
Representational systems
Noting your student's feedback
Heightened calibration
Anchoring
Coping with teacher burnouts
How to ask questions
Creating powerful internal images
Dealing with troubled students
Dealing with test anxiety
Dealing with a kinaesthestic child

This chapter is dedicated to two important authority figures in a child's life—the parent and the teacher. Depending on your memories of school, the word "teacher" will conjure up memories of an old curmudgeon or a warm and caring guide who introduced you to the wonderful ways of learning. The techniques outlined here are drawn from the NLP system of teaching and learning and are not taught in normal schools. A discerning parent reading this chapter will pick up lots of useful hints on how to connect more closely with his child.

Rapport

Rapport is essential for good teaching. The memories of your favourite teachers are invariably those of someone whom you could get along with, someone whom you felt understood your aspirations and hopes and the way you learned. Given that kind of an understanding, as the student, you would have wanted very much to reciprocate it by doing the best you could for that teacher. What would it be like if you could communicate that same sense of rapport to your students?

Rapport and motivation

Remember an area in which you excelled in, not because you liked the subject but because the teacher spoke your language? Think of other people that you liked. What do all of them have in common?

Connecting with others

What happens when you suddenly bumped into an old friend you haven't met in a long while and then arranged to have dinner with him? You are eager to meet him because of the experiences you have shared and you want to catch up with him, find out how he has been since you both left school. We feel most comfortable with people who are just like us. This can mean anything from race, colour or creed to similar values and beliefs. When you meet someone for the first time, you have less than 30 seconds to make an impact. In that vital 30 seconds, the future of your relationship is decided. Unfair, you may say. Research has shown that in most jury cases, the jury had made their final judgement based on the opening addresses made by the respective lawyers in the first 30 seconds of the trial.

When you meet someone for the first time, you are on trial. How swiftly you go about looking for a similarity will determine what happens next. One of the most effective ways of reducing differences is matching your body language to the other person's. When you meet a student for the first time, the degree to which you observe him and match and pace his physical movements would have a profound influence on how you can interact with him.

Ways of connecting nonverbally

- **Rapport**
  This is established when you communicate with each other and have found some similarities. In any encounter, 93% of the really meaningful communication is conveyed nonverbally.

- **Matching**
  To build rapport, try to duplicate your student's movements. If he keeps touching his forearm, you can touch your forearm or elsewhere unobtrusively. It is not necessary for the action to be observed by the student for it to be powerful.

- **Mirroring**
  If you are looking at yourself in a mirror, how would you move? In mirroring, when the other party moves their right arm, you move your left arm in a similar fashion. If you notice the rise and fall of your students' shoulders, use that rhythm to mirror his breathing rate. Another form of mirroring is repeating phrases and words that your student uses. This would show strongly that you care.

- **Crossover**
  Use one behaviour to match another behaviour, for example, tapping your foot to match your student's breathing rate.

- **Pacing**

  This occurs when you reaffirm the sense of connection you have already established. The other person feels their experience is being recognised and validated. You match and mirror the rhythm of their current actions, preferably nonverbally and, as the primary communicator in the relationship, you match the pace of change.

- **Leading**

  This is the point when you introduce the person to other experiences that would enrich his life. Taking a person from one state where they are not so well connected to all their resources, options and contexts of information to a desirable state of experience. Any leader has to be able to do this smoothly and elegantly. To lead the student, the teacher mirrors and matches her student until she paces him. When she is comfortably pacing the student, she is ready to lead him to the next state. One way to test if it is time for leading is to move an arm or leg and notice if the student does something similar.

  Leading is an effective way to build rapport between two people. However, undesirable or unusual behaviour should be paced differently so that the behaviour can be eliminated. In this case, crossover mirroring is used. That is, instead of matching the asthmatic breathing of a client, I would use my finger to tap and match as closely as possible his breathing rhythm.

- **Find similar interests**

  Talking about similar areas of interest is also a powerful way of building rapport. You may need to ask specific questions to determine a person's interests, such as:

  What hobbies do you have?

  What makes you happy?

  What would you buy that would make you feel good?

  The answers will give you lots of important information about the student. It will also provide a communication channel for both of you.

Activity

1. Pick a different student everyday to go through these exercises.
a. On the first day, match one student's behaviour for three minutes.
b. On the second day, mirror another students' behaviour for three minutes.
c. On the third day, cross mirror a third student for three minutes.
d. On the fourth day, practice pacing a student for three minutes.
e. On the fifth day, practice pacing and leading. When the student starts to follow your movements because you are in rapport, you have successfully completed this part.

2. Get into a conversation with a student. You want to persuade him to adopt a point of view that he is initially neutral to.
a. Mismatch and then persuade him for three minutes. What happens? How do you feel?
b. Enter into rapport with him and persuade him. Notice what happens. How do you feel? How does he feel?

Calibration

In order to do the previous processes elegantly, there are certain responses that you need to be able to note. The responses that really matter are the ones that the students do not say. When you talk to your student, do you listen to what they have to say and watch out for their nonverbal messages? Very often your student is giving you all the information that you need to move on. Calibration is all about listening and paying attention to the other person's verbal and nonverbal communication.

Sensory acuity

Being an effective communicator involves being aware of how and how well your communication is being received. It is useful to avoid attaching meanings to our observations until we have more information or the other person confirms our perceived meaning. What are the things you need to watch for?

• Breathing rate and depth
  Adjusting yourself to the breathing rate and depth is a powerful way to connect with someone.

- Facial expression
  Note how they use their brows, eyes, nose and mouth to create an impression or express their feelings.
- Body
  Note whether the shoulders and hips are level and whether the muscles are relaxed or tense.
- Gestures
  The different gestures, as well as their intensity and frequency, tell you what matters to the person and what does not.
- Pitch/Tone/Volume
  In most verbal cultures, these elements are extremely important. The same piece of information conveyed in different tones can mean very different things.
- Angle
  The tilt of the head can indicate an individual's major thinking style. For example, people who use their visual sense more often than the other senses normally look directly at a person. Auditories tilt their heads to one side.
- Speed of movement and speech
  How fast a person moves and talking is crucial. The sooner you can shift into his frequency, the faster connections are made.
- Type of movement
  Note how patterns of movement mark content shifts in conversations. You normally have 10 to 30 seconds to match movements or shifts.

Representational systems

We have five senses or information gathering channels through which we experience the outside world and send messages to the brain. These are the seeing, hearing, feeling, smelling and tasting senses.

After the sensory information enters our brain, the brain begins to process it in order to make sense of the world around us. To do this, it sorts this sensory information into important and less important information. Were you aware of the change in temperature on the back of your neck before being directed to notice an important piece of information? Probably not. Your brain deleted that piece of information from your awareness in order to protect you from information overload. If you suddenly became aware of the sensory information assaulting your senses at any given moment, your conscious mind would be quickly overwhelmed with too much information.

The human brain prioritizes in other ways as well. For example, humans generally prefer to use one hand over the other; we say they are either right-handed or left-handed. Likewise, some people prefer to gather information about the world through one sensory system over the others. In the earlier chapters, I gave a broad overview of these issues. In this chapter, I shall examine the critical areas in greater detail and demonstrate how you as the teacher can determine from your student's body or spoken language what particular sense he prefers to use.

Seeing

If a person favours the visual channel, he will say things like, "Your face looks familiar to me." Examples of words that characterize visuals include bright, dim, large, small, colour, vivid, shape, near, far, focused, clear, sparkle, perspective, flash, look, see, dimension, shine, reflect, magnify, etc. Famous visually-oriented people include scientists like Albert Einstein and artists like Pablo Picasso. Famous visual-kinaesthetics include successful business people like Donald Trump, creators like Walt Disney and top athletes like Jack Nicklaus.

Hearing

People who favour the hearing sense will say things like, "Your name rings a bell." Examples of hearing words are: loud, soft, whisper, shout, scream, resonate, harmony, talk, speak, sing, tone, pitch, vibrate and listen. Auditories include famous musicians like Mozart, the Beatles and Paul Simon.

Sensing

Kinaesthetic people need to be in touch with the world around them. The words that they like to use include: pressure, temperature, heavy, vibration, soft, cold, smooth. Famous kinaesthethics include all athletes—Jack Nicklaus, Tiger Woods, Jimmy Connors. Famous auditory-kinaesthetic people include Tom Peters and Bruce Springsteen.

Smelling

Some people have a highly developed sense of smell, such as perfumers.

Tasting

Others are excellent at taste, for example, wine tasters and chefs. They prefer to say, "This tastes like..."

It is important to note that this is not an either/or case. Nobody is visual *or* auditory *or* kinaesthetic. Everyone uses *all* of their senses, just that we prefer one or two over the others. So if you listen to the language a person uses and observe him, you will know what he prefers.

Activity
1. Get into a conversation with student. Identify their preferred sensory mode. When you are sure of it, replay it back to them.
2. Pick a subject to persuade a student with and do this by expressing the benefits of the topic in your student's preferred sensory terms.

Noting your student's feedback

Part of being able to calibrate, pace and lead involves being sensitive to the feedback received. Initially you may present the information in your students' preferred sensory modalities. However, if the message is not being communicated, you will need to change its presentation so that your students can understand it. By constantly checking to see if you are in or out of rapport, you can evaluate whether your message is getting through or whether you need to change your behaviour and language. If a student is uncomfortable or irritable, then you need to establish the reasons for his behaviour and change the situation. Sometimes one student's attitude can infect the whole class.

The figure below outlines the normal neurological patterns of organising information. When we wish to remember something visually, our eyes tend to look upper left. When we wish to imagine something visually, we tend to look towards the right. This is true for most individuals. Some people may be neurologically organised in reverse. The direction the eye focuses when the person tries to visually remember something is the site of visual memory. When something is imagined, the eyes move into the opposite direction, that is, to the upper right.

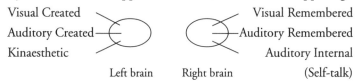

Visual Created		Visual Remembered
Auditory Created		Auditory Remembered
Kinaesthetic		Auditory Internal
Left brain	Right brain	(Self-talk)

Another way of checking the space where visual memories are located is by asking your child questions that involve visual memory.

- Visual remembered

  Seeing images of things seen before. Questions: "What colour is your mother's favourite dress?" or "What does your coat look like?"

- Visual created

  Seeing images never seen before or seeing things differently from the way they were seen before. Questions: "What would an orange hippopotamus with purple spots look like?" or "What would you look like from the other side of the room?"

- Auditory remembered

  Questions: "What does the national anthem sound like?" or "Remember what your favourite song sounds like?"

- Auditory created

  Question: "How would your favourite song sound if you played it backwards?"

- Kinaesthetic
  Question: "Remember a time when you experienced strong emotions about something?"

Heightened calibration

If a student suddenly turns a shade paler than normal, something is probably wrong with him. Picking up changes like this is more important than listening to verbal messages. When there is an incongruence between what the student is saying and his behaviour, it is another telltale sign. For example, if a student always twitches his fingers in a particular fashion before he answers "yes" and shakes his head when he is going to answer "no", then it is incongruent if he shakes his head to a "yes" question. The teacher needs to be sensitive to this inconsistency and follow it up.

There was a story about a student in an English class who used to write essays about how depressed and suicidal he was. In his essays, he described the physical and emotional abuse he was experiencing at home. The English teacher kept reprimanding him for his poor grammar but never asked about his feelings. Nine months later, the student committed suicide. The English teacher's response was, "I never knew that he had it so bad. He should have told me how bad the situation was." Teachers have to be more sensitive to their students' emotional states.

Anchoring

The competent teachers we had when we were students had the knack of anchoring us into positive states of learning. How is the teacher today going to deliberately produce the same effect?

There was an experiment done to illustrate the power of nonverbal communication. The students of a class decided to play a trick on their psychology professor. They all decided that they would pay attention to him only when he was in a particular part of the room. If he moved from that point, they would no longer pay any attention. Within the course of one lecture, they had trained him to stay and deliver his lecture from that corner of the room. In other words, the students anchored that particular response in the professor with their looks, low murmurs and the attention they gave him.

Before teachers learn to anchor a positive state in their students, they need to be able to anchor themselves in a positive fashion. We have outlined some methods below for anchoring positive states. You can also try the optimal state setting procedure in Chapter 10.

The more intense the experience, the more powerful the anchor. The more unique the stimulus, the more accurate it can reassess the desired state. Anchors are established in all representational systems. They can be fired overtly, by friends, or covertly, by television.

- Collapsing anchors
  Two anchors are fired at the same time to erase bad feelings. The positive anchor has to be amplified much more than the negative for the anchor to be effective.
- Chaining anchors
  A series of states are set up so one state leads to another for automation of states. For example, you can lead your student from frustration to intrigue to curiosity to enthusiasm.

Coping with teacher burnouts

I once worked with a teacher who developed hypertension because she was very involved with her teaching. When the principal asked her to do tasks that she felt was inappropriate, she would feel her blood pressure rise. She would also get headaches and feel dizzy. In the middle of a class, if she got passionate about a subject, the same thing would happen.

During her treatment, we created a disassociation anchor for her so that she can feel more distant about the situation and detach herself from it. Whenever she was in a potentially stressful situation, she was to mentally step back and look at the situation from behind a glass wall, then calmly observe what was being said and done from a disassociated state. The last step was to work out what she had to say and then step into her body to do it. After she practised this for 10 times, she tested it out in real life situations. She was pleased to note that her high blood pressure began to stabilise and her physician could slowly reduce her dose of medication.

We also wanted to create a different set of strategies for her to handle the different students. Before this exercise, she only had one speed when she taught: full speed ahead. However, such a teaching style was only appropriate at times; at other times, it was not. So we took her through exercise D: creating a positive state for teaching.

We had her recall a time when she felt the situation was more than she could presently handle. Then she put the situation aside. She next created a sphere about herself and remembered a time when she felt calm, strong, assured and focused when she was teaching (emotions like excited and enthused were not appropriate for her because she could readily access these resources and was not capable of putting a break on them). As she explore fully what she felt, heard, saw and what messages she was telling herself, she realised that she could teach this way too. We had her put this little package on her lower right side, i.e. position A.

While she was still in the sphere, we had her remember someone whom she respected and admired as a teacher. She ran through a brief scenario of how they would have coped with the situation resourcefully.

As she continued exploring, she realised that she had this belief that the only way to teach was this "Rah, Rah" style. This belief had been useful for her once. However, she now had within her powerful resources that would allow her to teach in a variety of ways effectively. As she continued investigating how this role model thought, felt, heard, saw and what messages she was telling herself, she began to wonder which qualities she could use herself. She soon realised that she was indeed using quite a few of the qualities. By adding on a few more qualities, she could teach in a style that she felt comfortable with again. She put this picture on her upper left hand side, i.e. position B.

Then we had her remember a time when she acted resourcefully and powerfully in a teaching situation in her life. As she explored this more fully, I could note her change in posture and her energy level rise. She became aware that she was telling herself messages such as "I enjoy the chance to share these ideas. I like seeing the excitement in their eyes when they see the connections." We had her put this picture in her lower left hand side, i.e. position C.

The second last stage was when we had her look at how she would have responded to the original situation if she had all the different strengths built in. She kept looking at her behaviour as it occurred outside her sphere and changed what she saw happening until it looked and sounded right. Then she left her sphere of influence to step into that picture and test whether it felt right. She stepped back and kept changing this picture until it felt right. When it was just right, she stepped back into her sphere of influence. She then put this picture in the upper right hand side of her sphere, i.e. position D.

B　　　　　　　　D

C　　　　　　　　A

After these, we had her roll her eyes gently and slowly as she experienced all of these states occurring one after another. After she had done it a few times both clockwise and anticlockwise, we had her recall the original situation. It was no longer distressful to her. In fact, she could not understand anymore why it had bothered her in the first place.

Activity

Create a positive anchor and a disassociation anchor for yourself and a high energy anchor for your child.

How to ask questions

In the course of your work, you need to be able to extract high quality information from your students. To do this, you need to be aware of what information you are seeking and which bits you are missing.

The first class of information that we miss out is when someone we are talking to makes references to something they think we are supposed to know. They delete information from the conversation and to understand them, we have to supply these missing information. Sometimes we get it right. Most often we don't. To recover this information, we have to ask them good questions. For example, your student might say, "I don't like this topic." You should ask, "What is it about this topic that you dislike?" This way, you can find out more precise information about your student's dislike. Here are other examples:

- This is better.   Better compared to what?
- I get little satisfaction.   What would be more satisfying?

At other times, we may encounter students with rigid ideas of what they can or cannot do. They may not even be aware that they are limiting their options. For example, if your student says, "I can never get it right," ask him, "You have never, ever got it right?" You could challenge his belief and ask him for a time when he had got something right. Sometimes, your student may say, "Nobody wants to gives me a chance." Challenge him and ask, "Nobody ever?" He should be able to recall at least one or two incidents when someone gave him a chance.

Students who feel victimised often say, "I can't do it." Ask them, "What would happen if you did?" Or "What stops you from doing this?" The teacher may find out that there are some family circumstances that may have contributed to this feeling. As a teacher, you should take note whenever some keywords appeared in the speech of your students, such as *never, all, none, nobody, everybody, can't, must, ought to.*

Sometimes, your students may try to make sense of something by personalising or distorting information to fit his own model of the world. For example, they may say, "I know that teacher hates me!" Ask, "How do you know for sure that she hates you?" If you probe further, you may find that the student has anchored a particular look from the teacher as hate because this is how her parents looked at her when they are displeased with her.

Creating powerful internal images

The following are two very powerful forms of questioning that will help your students create positive internal images.

- "What would happen if ... because ..."
  This is useful if your student uses words that expresses necessity (have to, must, shouldn't) or negative possibility (can't) while voicing an objection. If he says, "I can't do that" using an agreement tactic, ask him, "I know that you think you can't but what would happen if you can, because I know that you want to improve your grades."

- "Just suppose ..."
  This is more powerful than the previous one as it creates in your student's mind the desired internal images that you want. For example, "Just suppose for a moment that you could learn easily and effectively, how would you use all your spare time then?"

Activity

Create a powerful internal image for learning for your child/students.

Dealing with troubled students

Sometimes a student could be going through a bad patch and feel low or emotionally distraught. At such times, if you, his teacher, reprimand him for simple errors, he could end up playing the image repeatedly in his head. As a result of this constant replaying, he may feel mentally inadequate and be unable to function the moment he steps into class and sees you. He will associate with all his negative feelings while dissociating with the pleasant experiences he may have had with you.

To deal with this, you have to do the following procedure. Have the student sit comfortably on a chair. Then have him project on a screen a black and white movie of the incident where you reprimanded him. At this point, make sure that your student is still relaxed and comfortable. Then have him rewind and forward the picture at high speed until he feels totally neutral about it.

Next, ensure that the student feels good about the classes. You can have him recall a time when he felt good about something. As he connects with that experience by stepping inside the times when he felt good, he is asked to create a new experience where he sees himself enjoying your classes and you are smiling at him in that experience. When he can step into this new experience and see himself enjoying the class, the process stops. The whole experience can be anchored by having your student clench his fist.

Dealing with test anxiety

While many children experience some anxiety at the thought of sitting for tests, some students may become so distraught that they may no longer be able to calmly sit for tests and pass them. If you have identified such a child, you will need to remove the child from the class for a short period of time while working on the following procedure.

First, find strong influences that would provide a more powerful and positive anchor that would neutralise this reaction to tests. You may want to ask the student, "How do you feel about testing?" When the student demonstrates signs of discomfort, anchor this response on the right elbow. Then distract the student and test the anchor to make sure the same distress is evoked when she touches the right elbow.

Change the student's emotional state by having him talk about something that is important to him. At a time like this, having him evoke a memory of a time when he felt calm, confident and productive may also be useful. Ask your student if the intensity of this state is higher than the preceding negative state. When he is convinced that this state is positive, anchor this state on his left elbow. Then distract him by talking about something else and test the positive anchor by pressing the precise point on his left elbow. If he can readily call on the positive feelings, you can move on to the final step.

Press both anchors simultaneously, holding them for 10 seconds. Then release the negative anchor and continue holding on to the positive anchor. When the process is completed, check the efficacy of this procedure by noting the student's response to the word "test". If the student is neutral or unmoved by the word, then the procedure has been effective.

If the student experiences any discomfort, this means that the procedure is not successful. You will repeat the procedure but this time, stack on more positive anchors. Have the student recall more than one suitable positive occasion while you keep pressing his left elbow. The process of activating both anchors is repeated and the student is again checked for any anxiety at the mention of the trigger word.

Dealing with a kinaesthetic child

When you deal with a kinaesthetic student, you need to realise that the active child may not be able to access a behaviour you desire. This is because by nature or by nurture, he has become anchored to a sequence of energetic behaviour that is inappropriate within the classroom.

When you meet the student, you need to point out the behaviour that she considers unacceptable in terms of visual, auditory, kinaesthetic components. It must be done so that at the end of the process, you are able to model the behaviour. This is when the questioning model outlined earlier comes in useful. A transcript is enclosed to illustrate the ideas. (*T* stands for teacher, Miss Chan, *D* stands for student, David.)

T : David, I have noticed that you often get restless, fidgety and then start running around in class.

D : Yes, Miss Chan. I know you're aware that I also throw paper pellets at the other students when they are not looking. You are not going to punish me, are you? (a little concerned)

T : No, David (reassuringly). This is to find out what makes you restless. David, are you aware that you get restless and fidgety in class? Are you aware that you distract the other students as well?

D : I do know that certain classes make me get restless. But I do not know that I distracted the other students.

T : Are you also aware that when you get restless, you also start fidgeting in your chair and moving around the classroom?

D : I know that when I get restless, I do move around a bit. But I do not know that I got out of my chair. (David is a bit surprised. Miss Chan's words made him realise that he does indeed have such an action.)

T : David, what makes you restless in class?

D : I don't know. I just get kind of fidgety when I sit down for too long.

T : How long before you get fidgety, David?

D : I am not sure, Miss Chan. It just seems like a long time.

T : (She makes him re-experience the state in order to get more high quality information.) Remember the last time you got restless, David? (In a soothing voice that maintains rapport) It may be today or yesterday.

D : (David looks up to his left and his eyes flicker a little before speaking) It was yesterday during Mathematics. It was so boring.

T : How did you know when to feel bored David? What did you see, hear or feel that made you go, "Yes, it's time to get bored." (humorously to remain in rapport)

D : First, the teacher's voice went on for too long. Then I started to feel an uncomfortable sensation in my stomach. Next, I want to move.

T : Have you ever sat down for a long time and not wanted to move?

D : Yes, when I am playing with my clay and making funny shapes.

T : What happens then?

D : Well, as I work on the shapes and feel them grow beneath my hands, I feel so good that I don't want to move. (David is saying that when he gets a good feeling after sitting for a long time, he does not fidget. When he gets an uncomfortable feeling in his stomach, he starts to get fidgety.)

T : How would you like to feel when you are in class instead of what you presently feel, David?

D: I like to feel that what is happening in class is fun. I don't want to feel so fidgety.

T: Would you like to be curious about what happens next in class?

D: Yes! Yes! (nodding profusely)

T: After feeling curious, what else would you like to feel? How about relaxed and calm?

D: Yup.

T: How about the next state? Would you like to feel the way you feel when you are working on your clay?

D: Yup, that's cool.

T: How about feeling really relaxed and calm when you think of being in a class?

D: Yeah, but I don't know if that works.

(Miss Chan decides to use the following technique of creating chaining anchors, starting from hyperactivity to curiosity to relaxed to focused concentration and to future pace.)

T: Well, David, I want you to think of a time when you were really fidgety in class. As you see the picture of yourself, step into your body and experience it fully. (As David accesses that state, she watches for the fidgets to start before she anchors that state on the last knuckle of the tight hand. She then distracts him by asking him about his favourite games. As he begins to tell her, she tests the anchor by pressing the first anchor. He starts to get fidgety.)

T: David, now I want you to remember a time when you were really curious about something. As you recall, I want you to become aware of what you felt, heard and smelled at that time. (As David accesses this state, she presses his third knuckle at the height of the experience. She then tests the anchor by distracting him and firing it.)

T: David, I want you to remember a time when you were really relaxed and comfortable. As you remember that period, I want you to become more aware of what you felt, heard and smelled at that time as you

171

experience that state of relaxation now. (As David accesses this state, she presses the second knuckle at the height of the experience. She then tests the anchor by distracting him and firing it.)

T : David, now remember a time when you were focused on your clay as you felt them grow beneath your hands (By reusing his own words, she deepens his state.) As you remember and experience that period of focused attention, I want you to become more aware of what you saw, felt, heard and smelled at that time. (As David accesses this state, she presses his first knuckle at the height of the experience. She then tests the anchor by distracting him and firing it.)

T: David, now I want you to remember a time when you were really focused and attentive in class and you can see yourself doing it now as you look into the future. As you remember and experience that period, I want you to become more aware of what you felt, heard and smelled at that time. (As David accesses this state, she presses his thumb knuckle at the height of the experience. She then tests the anchor by distracting him and firing it. Finally, she completes the process by firing the anchors one after another from the knuckle on the last finger to the thumb knuckle. David experiences the sensations of the different states. Miss Chan is careful not to trigger off two states at the same time. So, as her fingers move from one knuckle to the other, the preceding state is quickly passed over. If David is required to access the state of calm focused concentration, he can press the first knuckle himself and reassess the experience.)

The above is an example of some of the principles in action. I believe that the more fully teachers enter the mindset of their students, the more effective teaching is going to be. The old method of rote learning will have less use in the world as more sophisticated methods of processing and storing information are adopted.

GLOSSARY

Aggresive-style response (pg 125)
A style where the speaker forces his thoughts and views on the listener.

Anchoring (pg 134, 162)
An easily reproducible state change (like a fist) that allows one to access a desired state (e.g. happy).

Assertive-style response (pg 126)
A style where the speaker firmly and politely presents his views.

Emotional Intelligence (pg 10)
An individual's capacity to acknowledge and use his emotions meaningfully.

Imprint period (pg 15)
The critical time frame in which an imprint is formed.

Injunctions (pg 20)
Negative, restricting messages about behaviour issued by parent to child.

Lifeskills (pg 128-130)
Skills necessary to function in life.

Modelling (pg 16)
Taking on values of authority figures and behaving like them.

Neuro-Linguistic Programming (pg 16)
Using language and sensory inputs to change one's experience.

Passive-style response (pg 124)
A style characterised by avoiding conflict, being subservient and not acknowledging one's emotions.

Permissions (pg 20-28)
Positive, liberating messages from parent to child.

Rapport (pg 154)
Reducing differences and increasing similarities between people.

Strokes (pg 59-62)
The way we recognise and acknowledge someone.

Systems approach (pg 149)
Analysing people's behaviour in terms of group dynamics.

BIBILIOGRAPHY

EMOTIONAL INTELLIGENCE

Drego, Pearl. *Happy Family–Parenting Through Family Rituals.* Bombay: Alfreruby Publishers, 1994.

Goleman, Daniel. *Emotional Intelligence.* Bantam Books, 1995.

Rollins, Catherine E. and Dargatz, Jan. *Building Self-esteem And Confidence In Yourself And Your Child.* New York: Galahad Books, 1994.

Schmitz, Connie and Hipp, Earl. *A Teacher's Guide To Fighting Invisible Tigers.* USA: Free Spirit Publishing Company, 1987.

LEARNING AND TEACHING

Kline, Peter. *The Everyday Genius.* USA: Great Ocean Publishers Inc., 1988.

NEURO-LINGUISTIC PROGRAMMING

Nage, C. Van, Reese, Edward J. and Maryann, and Siudzinski, Robert, *Mega Teaching And Learning.* USA: Metamorphous Press, 1985.

Grinder, Michael, *Righting The Educational Conveyor Belt.* USA: Metamorphous Press, 1989.

Dilts, Robert. *Strategies Of Genius Vol 1.* USA: Meta Publications, 1994.

Dilts, Robert. *Strategies Of Genius Vol 2.* USA: Meta Publications, 1994.

PREPARING FOR THE REAL WORLD

Kiyosaki, Robert T. and Bennet, Hal Zina. *Do You Need To Go To School To Be Rich And Happy?* Singapore: Heinemann Asia, 1994.

THE BRAIN AND ITS POTENTIAL

Armstrong, Thomas. *7 Kinds of Smart*. A Plume Book, 1993.

Buzan, Tony. *Make the most of your mind*. Pan Books, 1988.

Dennison, Paul E. and Hargrave, Gail. *E-K for kids*. Edu-Kinesthetics, 1985.

Doman, Glenn and Doman, Janet. *How To Multiply Your Baby's Intelligence*. New York: Avery Publishing Group, 1994.

Doman, Glenn, Doman, Janet and Aisen, Susan. *How To Give Your Baby Encyclopedic Knowledge*. New York: Avery Publishing Group, 1994.

Ostrander, Sheila, Schroeder, Lynn and Ostrander, Nancy. *Super Learning 2000*. New York: Delacorte Press, 1994.

Waas, Lane Longino. *Imagine That*. California: Jalmar Press, 1991.

Wenger, Win. *Beyond O.K.* USA: Psychogenics Press, 1979.

Wenger, Win. *How To Increase Your Intelligence*. New York: D.O.K. Publishers, 1987.

MORE ABOUT THE AUTHOR

A professor in the Youngson Institute of Colleges Worldwide and a Neuro-Linguistic Programming Trainer, Dr. Sundardas D. Annamalay has conducted workshops on Emotional Intelligence for the SDU and the Ministry of Home Affairs, as well as workshops on Stress and Personal Empowerment in Malaysia, Australia, Taiwan and Sri Lanka. He regularly holds seminars in schools for students on Accelerated Learning and EI and for teachers on NLP, teaching and stress management.

Dr. Sundardas has been a trainer to organisations such as SIMEX, FOREX, ABN-AMRO Bank, Asia Breweries, Asia Matushita Electric (S) Pte. Ltd., Batey Ads Group, Business Trends and MPH. He had worked with the Transactional Analysis Association of Singapore, the Woodbridge Nurses Association and the National Counselling Conference.

Dr. Sundardas is the author of *The Asian Woman's Guide to Health, Beauty and Vitality*, *Awakening the Genius in Your Child*, and is the co-author of *The Pindlahr Techniques*.

In 1994 Dr. Sundardas was awarded the Dr. Yudhvir Singh Memorial Award by a government-backed organisation in India for his work in Natural Medicine. In 1997 he was listed in the 13th edition of *The International Who's Who of Intellectuals*, *The International Who's Who of Professionals* and in the 5th edition of *The International Directory of Distinguished Leadership for Outstanding Service in the Field of Alternative Medicine*.

His academic background includes a Bachelor of Science in Physics (Singapore), an honours degree in Natural Science (Australia), and a Ph.D. in Natural Science (USA). He also has a doctorate in Naturopathy (USA).

Dr. Sundardas is currently running a natural therapy centre in Singapore, helping children and adults. You can visit his centre's website at http://www.NaturalTherapies.com.